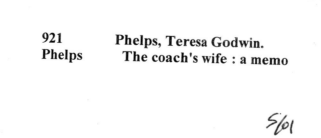

THE COACH'S WIFE

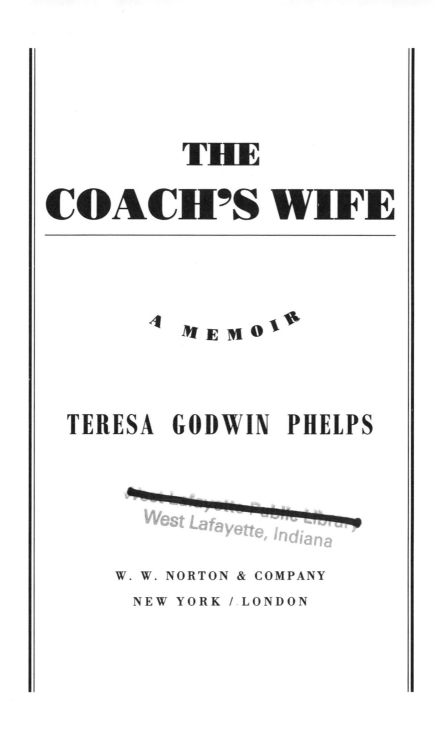

THE
COACH'S WIFE

A MEMOIR

TERESA GODWIN PHELPS

W. W. NORTON & COMPANY

NEW YORK / LONDON

The text of this book is composed in 11/13.5 New Baskerville
with the display set in Poster Bodoni and Bodoni Bold Condensed
Composition and manufacturing by The Haddon Craftsmen, Inc.
Book design by Jo Anne Metsch

Library of Congress Cataloging-in-Publication Data

Phelps, Teresa Godwin.
The coach's wife: a memoir / Teresa Godwin Phelps
p. cm.
1. Phelps, Richard. 2. Phelps, Teresa Godwin. 3. Athletic
coaches' wives—United States—Biography. I. Title.
GV884.P45A3 1994
796.323'092—dc20
[B]

ISBN 0-393-03470-4

W. W. Norton & Company, Inc., 500 Fifth Avenue, New York, N.Y. 10110
W. W. Norton & Company Ltd., 10 Coptic Street, London WC1A 1PU

1 2 3 4 5 6 7 8 9 0

For my husband and my children—
without whom, nothing.

C O N T E N T S

THE COACH'S WIFE

P R O L O G U E

Some years ago I wanted to write a book called *The Lovely Wives* about women, such as me, who are married to men in sports. It was to be about "lovely wives"—as TV commentators invariably call us—women whose lives are intimately affected by the vicissitudes of sports. We are expected to be present at all the games, we sometimes lead the cheering (some have even been seen dancing on the dugout), we welcome sports (personified as players, fans, sportswriters, coaches) into our homes. But after the big game, win or lose, the door slams shut and we stand waiting outside that notorious "no-woman's-land," the locker room. The lovely wives are so connected to the day-to-day life of a sport, but are nonetheless outsiders, symbolically barred from the inner sanctum, the holy place where victory is celebrated and rewarded, where defeat is mourned and healed.

As for the title, I had a recurring fantasy: during a nationally televised basketball game, a TV commentator says, "There's Digger Phelps's lovely wife in the stands." The camera pans to me as

I slowly turn to face the television audience and smile broadly at the camera with a few blackened teeth. Many coaches' wives *are* lovely, but sports announcers use it as if it were a single word from the novel *1984*—"lovelywife"—used to stand for a certain kind of woman: trivial, irrelevant, interchangeable.

To collect data for *The Lovely Wives*, I sent questionnaires to coaches' and athletes' wives all over the country. Many returned them, and some of those women still ask me if I'm going to write that book. I never did write it. My life moved on: I went back to school for an advanced degree, wrote a dissertation, and then took a job teaching in a law school. The only writing for which I had time was that connected to my career as a college professor. My own years as a lovelywife passed and I never wrote *The Lovely Wives*.

A few years ago, I decided to turn *The Lovely Wives* into this book, my own story, one I felt more competent to tell. I waited for my life as a coach's wife to end so that the story would have closure. My husband and I discussed his leaving coaching and taking up some other work, a second career, perhaps something in government service. My life as a lovelywife would soon be over. But his last year as a coach came more quickly than we expected and not in the way we would have chosen. That final year, nonetheless, is the frame upon which I hang my story of life as a coach's wife, the lens through which the past must be seen. The book's structure is that of experience and reverie: of the present informed and interpreted by the past. It is a story that is both individual and universal, one in which I believe many coaches' wives, perhaps many women, will find fragments of their own stories. In a way, this book is for all those women who returned the questionnaires and said they hoped that I would write that book. I know that it is not all their stories, only one—mine. But it is at least one.

Like many women, coaches' wives tend to be a silent lot, speaking only in platitudes and clichés about their husbands and their sports. They reveal the pleasant, upbeat side of college sports in their answers to the typical questions that fans and sportswriters invariably ask: What is he like after a loss? Do you get to go to *all* the games? But there's another side to this whole business that is not so pretty—and the ugliness can take many shapes. Sports, unfortunately, is a place where meanness and violence rub shoulders with kindness and generosity. It may be time for new questions to be asked and answered.

My friend Susan Penders, wife of the head basketball coach at Texas, once dared to speak out about fan harassment. Opposing fans, knowing she was the coach's wife, had yelled abusive, sexually explicit things at her during a game. When Susan complained, loud and clear, the resulting brouhaha culminated in columns in *USA Today*. Beau Dure, a senior at Duke and an editor of the school newspaper, condoned the behavior and claimed that crowd abuse added harmless fun to the games. Essentially, if you pay the price of a ticket, you can yell anything you want, including (and this was his example) calling Notre Dame's David Rivers "Buckwheat." Susan wrote the opposing view, saying that she was appalled (and hurt) by universities that countenanced fan harassment—racial, sexual, whatever. Good for Susie! She had courage, and I'm sure she met with plenty of criticism about a coach's wife keeping her mouth shut, or "if you can't stand the heat stay out of the kitchen."

When I reflect now on my twenty-five years as a coach's wife, what memory brings back from that time is not the upheaval of the final year, but a kaleidoscope of people and events that help to give it shape and meaning. When I look back on myself at the start of it all, imagining a future that is already long past, I realize how little I knew or understood, how naive my expectations were, and how much I have come to learn.

PART ONE

SPRING

1990

"When I use a word," Humpty-Dumpty said in a rather scornful tone, "it means just what I choose it to mean, neither more nor less."

"The question is," said Alice, "whether you *can* make words mean so many different things."

"The question is," said Humpty-Dumpty, "which is to be Master—that's all."

—*Through the Looking Glass*

1

I t wasn't April Fools' Day, nor was it the Ides of March. It was, instead, a typical gray, cold, late March day in South Bend, Indiana. Not a day for fools or murders, but something in between. Our nineteenth Notre Dame basketball season had recently ended. The season began with much promise, saw more than its share of peaks and valleys, and concluded just a week before with a dismal showing against Virginia in the first round of the NCAA tournament in Richmond, the old capital of the Confederacy. With ten minutes left in that game, I sat in the stands praying that Joe Fredrick and Jamere Jackson would begin to play better. Both seniors had experienced an incredibly up-and-down year. "Please," I whispered to whatever deity watches over basketball, "let them play the way we all know they can. Let them finish the year up." Then I added, just to stay honest, "For *me,* as well as for them."

Behind me the athletic director, Dick Rosenthal, and the executive vice-president of Notre Dame, Father Beauchamp, sat making tentative arrangements for their private plane to take them that night to a golf course farther south. They sounded relieved that, given the team's ineptness on the floor, they probably would not have to stick around and watch us play the next round. My prayers went unanswered and they caught their plane, apparently too rushed to stop off in the locker room to console the disappointed players.

The rest of us—the team, my husband, Digger Phelps, his assistant coaches, and I—caught a commercial flight the next morning, St. Patrick's Day, back to South Bend to face life without basketball games or practice for the next six months. As I sat in the airport lounge, I stuffed a plastic bag filled with green noses into the bottom of my carry-on. The day before we left for Richmond, I had purchased twenty green rubber clown noses, which were sold as a fund-raiser by Logan Center, a South Bend school for the mentally disabled. I had planned to hand them out to the team and coaches on St. Patrick's Day. As I waited for our plane in the Richmond airport, however, I decided that the long faces on Joe, Jamere, Keith Tower, LaPhonso Ellis, and the other players would not be improved by green noses. As for my husband, for whom St. Patrick's Day was usually second only to Christmas for celebration, his sense of humor was perilously thin. Beating Virginia had been a chance to redeem a mediocre season and his disappointment at the poor showing etched his face. No green nose for him either.

When we arrived at home late that afternoon, I gave St. Patrick's Day one more try. "Shall we go to the Reillys' party?" Frank Reilly, the former dean of the business school, and his wife, Therese, had an annual St. Pat's Day bash that we always missed because we were playing in a basketball tournament. "I told them we couldn't make it, but I'm sure they won't mind if we show up anyway."

"I'm too tired, Terry. Why don't you just pick up a movie and we'll stay in?" This unwillingness to socialize after a loss was a significant change. Even after a gut-wrenching tournament loss to Brigham Young University a few years ago, when Danny Ainge stole the ball with 8 seconds left in the game and hit the buzzer shot to beat us (after we had led by 10), Dick was willing to go out with friends when we returned to South Bend.

"No problem," I replied. "I'll get a pizza. Sausage for you?"

I arrived home an hour later with a large pizza, sausage and peppers (the peppers for me), and a video of *Gaslight*. Dick was sound asleep on the sofa in the TV room, fatigue showing plainly on his face, his more-gray-than-black hair a smudge above his closed eyes. He was nearing his fiftieth birthday and it showed. How much longer is he going to do this to himself? I thought. At least he'd be able to get a little rest before he left at the end of the month for the annual coaches' convention during the Final Four tournament. I picked the sausage off a few slices of pizza and watched Charles Boyer trying to drive Ingrid Bergman crazy. He should have become a basketball coach, I thought. That would have done it.

January 1974. UCLA, perennial national champion, has won 88 straight games. On the home court at Notre Dame, we are down 11; 3 minutes and 21 seconds remain on the clock. The crowd is subdued, content that at least it hasn't been a blowout. Folks who leave games early to beat the traffic are already on their way to the parking lot. Dick calls a time-out and changes the press, putting John Shumate up front and Gary Brokaw in the back. Shu scores, UCLA misses the change and Shu easily intercepts Tom Curtis's pass to Bill Walton and goes in to score again—we are down by 7. The students in the stands, silenced by UCLA's apparently insurmountable lead, begin to get back into the game: "We are . . . N——D" begins as a murmur and swells to a roar. Adrian Dantley steals the inbounds pass and goes in for a lay-up—down 5. "Dee-fense, dee-fense," the crowd screams. UCLA misses and Brokaw scores—down 3. Keith Wilkes charges, we get the ball, and Brokaw scores again—down 1. UCLA turns the ball over on a walk and double-teams Brokaw who has scored the last two baskets. Gary passes to Dwight Clay in the corner and Dwight, earning his nickname "the Iceman," hits from the right corner— up 1. With 20 seconds left, UCLA, the best team ever in college basketball, fails to score. The ball bounces and bounces off the rim as at least three shots go amiss. Shu finally gets the rebound and with 2 seconds left sends the ball high into the air. We win 71–70 on national television and the campus and town erupt.

I stand paralyzed at my seat in the stands and watch with a mixture of exhilaration and anxiety as thousands of frenzied students pour out onto the floor and clamber on shoulders to cut down the nets. They hoist Dwight Clay, Ray Martin, and Gary Novak up and, as they had prophetically rehearsed at practice the day before, they unhook the nets from the curved prongs. It is a moment of heightened unreality and there is something quite frightening about the uncontrolled hysteria on the floor; mobs are quick to turn on those whom they zealously celebrate. And there is also something quite wonderful at this unified show of joy over a team doing the unexpected, playing over their heads, David felling Goliath.

We had planned a postgame party—for a mere hundred or so friends—but our house becomes the stopping-off point for every fan or student who feels the need to congratulate Dick in person. Hundreds of people walk through our house, feast on my carefully prepared buffet, and relive the game. One friend, a conservative priest, waltzes with my mother-in-law across our living room, his face beaming above his clerical collar. Long after midnight, when every edible thing in the house has been made into party food and consumed, I fall into bed, not knowing whether to laugh or cry, to the sound of people still celebrating downstairs.

Gaslight came to its inevitable end. Ingrid Bergman survived. And so shall I, I thought as I brushed pizza crumbs off my lap, rewound the film, and slipped off to bed, leaving my Joseph Cotton still sleeping on the couch to his dream of a different ending to the game against Virginia. That was Dick's only reaction to a loss: a night of replaying the game as he slept—the turnover that didn't happen, the foul shot that went in, his game plan perfectly executed. He had accumulated 409 wins in twenty years as a head coach to help him sleep; but it was his 178th loss, the one to Virginia, that haunted his dreams that night.

The 1989–90 season had ended, as so many do, not with a bang but a whimper. Yet even after twenty-five years as a coach's wife, one who yearns for the end of the season, I never found the suddenness of the ending easy. The basketball season, for good or ill, structures your life completely: meals are planned around practices, social life revolves around games, trips out of town are for basketball games, and vacations or even days off—well, there aren't any, ever, between October and April. After a few months, you settle into this kind of life and then it's suddenly over, finished off in the final seconds of a close tournament game.

Every season, for every team but one, ends with a loss. If you win the last game but don't get a postseason bid, that's a loss—you are not among the "elect." We'd experienced that only twice in twenty years. If you make a tournament, and we'd seen eighteen of those, you play only until you lose, unless you happen to be the one team that wins the national title. So no matter what, there's always a letdown, a sense of things not turning out as well as they could have. And it is always sudden: one day the intensity of preparing for the next big game, the next day the games and practices that have controlled your life for half a year end.

The end of the nineteenth Notre Dame season was unusually welcome. The season was not a disaster, merely disappointing. Our best player was ineligible academically for half the season, the schedule was unmerciful, and we struggled to win 16 games and lose 12—a decent record but marginal for a postseason bid. The same tough schedule that beat us up all year, on the other hand, resulted in a bid to the NCAA tournament.

The Sunday when the NCAA bids came out, I was with some friends, Mary and Fred Ferlic and John and Mary Houck, in Chicago. We had all traveled to Chicago on Saturday for the DePaul game, our final regular-season game. Dick returned earlier on Sunday to South Bend where he and the team on campus anxiously watched the big board of NCAA matchups unfold on CBS, just as he had done fourteen times in his eighteen previous years at Notre Dame. I stayed in Chicago with the Houcks and the Ferlics to listen to Kiri Te Kanawa sing in concert and to eat dinner in Greektown, welcome distractions from the tension of the season. In a bar on Halsted Street, Mary Ferlic smiled sweetly as she walked up to the bar. "Would you mind changing the channel to CBS so we can see who goes to the NCAA tournament?" she said to the bartender. "DePaul might get in," she added as bait. We always designate Mary to ask for things; she never takes no for an answer.

"They better," the bartender growled as he flipped the channel. "They beat Notre Dame last night."

"Really?" Mary replied innocently and winked at us. Surrounded by Chicagoans, likely DePaul fans, we were keeping a low profile. DePaul had a better season record than Notre Dame, but our schedule was much tougher (which gave us a higher "power rating"), so it was a toss-up as to who would receive an NCAA bid. Dick had had fourteen seasons of 20 or more wins—including the six previous years—so a bid was not usually in question. My back was stiff with tension and my stomach so nervous that I almost fell off the bar stool. "Does Brent Musburger have to drag this out like he's doing *Hamlet*?" I asked. " 'To go, or not to go, that is the question.' "

After what felt like hours, Notre Dame's name appeared matched against Virginia in the Eastern Regional; DePaul's name never showed up. The angry responses from the bartender and patrons made it clear that Chicago was not pleased. We silenced our cheers, made surreptitious thumbs-up gestures to each other, and adjourned to the Greek Islands for some spanakopita.

During dinner I went through my mental checklist: cancel anything scheduled for the end of the week, call the kennel for the dog, pick up clothes at the cleaner's, pack for the long weekend in Richmond, find out which of my children would be going and when, contact relatives and friends to see who would be there, buy twenty green noses at Logan Center. I was too superstitious to make a single plan to travel to a tournament game before we received a bid. If I made any arrangements, we wouldn't get a bid—I was sure of that. Luckily it was spring break so I didn't need to re-schedule classes, although I had to remember to take along some of the eighty student legal briefs that needed grading over the break. And all Dick had to do was watch hours of tapes of the teams in our bracket, feverishly work out game plans, and prepare the team.

All that anticipation and preparation only to lose in the first round. I kept telling myself that thirty-one other teams also lost in the first round but my misery was not tempered by all that company. The season was not bad enough to contemplate calling in Dr. Kevorkian, but sadly below fan expectations, and the loss to Virginia had provided the impetus for a new round of second-guessing. More than that, a chilly climate had descended on the Phelpses at Notre Dame, and we were not prepared for it. The season, in fact, was so trying that it prompted my children to write a letter to the school paper. It read:

Dear Editor:

In 1971 we packed all our toys and headed West from New York. We found our new home in South Bend, Indiana. Dad's dream finally came true—he would be the Head Basketball Coach at Notre Dame.

We were all too young to really remember his first few seasons at the A.C.C. Dwight Clay's shot to break U.C.L.A.'s 88 game winning streak was the first of many memorable upsets. We even got to celebrate in the locker room after the game.

Through grade school, high school, the many cold winters, Dad's players all coming and graduating, Dad's winning basketball seasons, and the trips to the NCAA tournament, we made South Bend our home. All of the people in the town and school have always been a part of our "family." Sure there have been some frustrating times with Dad losing games or Dad not being home because of his busy schedule, but South Bend and Notre Dame have always been our home.

Now one of us is a 1987 Notre Dame graduate, one will graduate from Toledo University next March, and the youngest will graduate from Notre Dame next May. Unfortunately, we all can't get home to see all of the basketball games. But this season, Dad's 19th season, we feel we need to be here more than ever. Why? Because of the unsupporting boos during the introductions. (Even after the Irish upset Syracuse under a masterful game plan.) We find ourselves clapping alone and putting our arms around our Mother, who tries to justify the stupidity of the boos. We have been to many games in the last 19 years at home and on the road. We can understand why there wouldn't be loud cheers for Dad at the opponent's home, but at our home? Maybe there is too much emphasis on winning, don't you think? Imagine being at the place you call home, the place where no matter how bad things get you can always turn to, and then your "friends" and "family" turn against you.

Dad doesn't even know we are writing this, and honestly we have never discussed the boos. We are not asking for sympathy; rather, those of you who aren't clapping for your head basketball coach, ask yourselves if you realize what you are really doing. We are sure you don't, but if you do, maybe Notre Dame's family theme is a false realization, and the only home the Phelps family has is just the five of us.

Karen, Rick, and Jennifer Phelps
Feb. 26, 1990

Going public with such a letter was naive and I would have discouraged it had I known about it beforehand. My children's letter, although their courage and loyalty filled me with pride, troubled me. They put their hearts on their sleeves for all the campus to see and to ridicule.

But ridicule was the furthest thing from my children's minds. In their letter they addressed the Notre Dame they knew growing up, the place where they had been unconditionally loved and accepted, welcomed as members of the family. Our lives and their childhoods had been so intertwined with Notre Dame that they seemed indivisible. Between the lines of their letter were memories—events both trivial and momentous. Like all the times that Dottie Van Paris, Dick's secretary, let Karen and Jenny play "secretary" in Dick's office during practice. Like the times they sneaked into Ara Parseghian's office to steal candy from the candy dish on his desk. Ara always played along: "Where could all my candy have gone?" he'd say loudly. "Could I have eaten it all myself?" Like the times when Colonel Jack Stephens, assistant to then–athletic director Moose Krause, played with the three little Phelpses in their dad's office while he was busy elsewhere. Once Jack bandaged them with yards and yards of gauze as if they had broken limbs and cracked heads. Then he helped them startle everyone who dared to peek in the office. They giggled for days after that.

And they wept for days after Father Bill Toohey's death. Bill and Sister Jane Pitz of the Campus Ministry staff were integral parts of our lives. I came to know Bill and Jane because their Campus Ministry office in the library concourse provided free coffee. The office (and the coffee) became my retreat from endless hours of studying and writing my dissertation in my fourth-floor carrel. Bill and Jane prepared Jenny for her First Communion and celebrated afterwards with us at our house. More than that, they became our good friends. The Mass over which Bill regularly presided, the 12:15 each Sunday, became our family Mass. Along with a few dozen other weekly attenders, we gathered in an intimate group in the west transept of the vast Sacred Heart Church, otherwise filled with tourists and leftover football fans. Bill, Jane, Father Fitz, and others on Bill's staff had a way of pulling us into their circle of worship. Bill literally drew the congregation into a circle of worship when he, with his silver hair gleaming above a purple or green surplice, would step down from the altar to join hands with the congregation across the aisle for the singing of "Our Father." And when Karen came home upset from her Catholic elementary school because she had been told that she could not serve on the altar, that only *boys* could assist at Mass, it was Bill who told her she could serve on *his* altar anytime.

This was the Notre Dame to whom that brave letter went—the Dotties, Jacks, Bills, Janes, Fitzes. The mix of love and compassion—the stunning ability to be present in each other's lives in times of joy, of celebration, of grief, of mourning, in good seasons and in bad—this was the Notre Dame to whom my children wrote. It was the only Notre Dame they knew—until now. That the warmth was rapidly giving way to chill was something they refused to believe.

But it was true. Fans in the basketball arena booed when Dick's name was announced before a game. I would stand, the backs of my knees pressed hard against the seat, and fight futilely against my fatal tendency to blush, which announced far too much about my feelings. I began to arrive at games slightly late so that I would miss the introductions. The sudden public turnaround hurt like hell, but I smiled all the way through it. Dick's local South Bend and Notre Dame public image as basketball coach—boyish, flashy, charismatic—had mysteriously changed from endearing to annoying. I began to wait for the other shoe to drop.

On that gray, cold, late March afternoon, just a little over a week after the loss to Virginia in Richmond, I arrived home from my office in the law school and read Bill Gleason's column in the local paper, the *South Bend Tribune*. Referring to the avalanche of pro and con Digger letters that appeared during the season, Gleason wrote: "Digger doesn't need defending. He has given Notre Dame exactly the kind of basketball team that the administration wants. . . . His players graduate. His players do not end up in substance abuse programs. And part of the truth is that Digger doesn't recruit very many great high school players. He can't because too many great players could not even approach Notre Dame's academic standards. Let's look at the record, as the politicians say. Digger's record is excellent. He is a winner." I felt a surge of relief. We loved Notre Dame and had made it our life. After the roller coaster season, it was reassuring to know that the world remained sane, with winning in perspective. Basketball remained part of the academic enterprise of a potentially great university. The basketball program, with its integrity and consistency, could even contribute to that greatness. People would begin to remember that— Gleason did—and next year would be better.

Then Dick walked in, looking a little shaken. "Nice article," I said and handed him the paper. He glanced at Gleason's column quickly and began to shake his head and chuckle softly. "Something's wrong," I observed.

"You might say that." He had met with Dick Rosenthal, the athletic director, and "he told me that next year was my last, that they really wanted to fire me now but that they would let me coach next year since it was my twentieth season."

It took me a moment to respond; I thought that I had misheard what he had said. As his words slowly penetrated, I stepped toward him and put my arms around him. "I don't get it," I finally said. "What have you done wrong?"

"That was exactly my question. He said that they didn't like my style of play and that the students weren't buying enough tickets. He said that other schools, such as Duke and Arkansas, were consistently in the top twenty and we weren't. This and that. Nothing definite or precise. They just want a change."

"They?"

"Father Malloy, Father Beauchamp, and Rosenthal. The big three."

"What on earth did you say?"

"I said that I had certainly planned to coach the Ellis, Bennett, Sweet, Tower group through their senior year, that is, for the next two years. They're one of the best recruiting classes I've had. If they can all stay eligible, we should have a great team in two years. In fact, I think I'd like to coach at Notre Dame for five more years until I'm fifty-five. Rosenthal said I could meet with Malloy and Beauchamp, but that the three of them had made up their minds."

Dick left the next day for the Final Four in Denver and the annual basketball coaches convention. He was on the National Association of Basketball Coaches (NABC) board of directors and chaired the NABC legislative committee that proposed rule changes to the NCAA at its national convention. The Final Four for him was a constant crush of meetings, as he was one of the college coaches who had been in basketball long enough to assume responsibility for its future direction. He tried to keep his attention focused on his professional responsibilities; he cared about college basketball and had worked for years to instill some integrity into the system. When he called me from Denver, though, he said that he was having trouble keeping his heart in it. "I don't know, Terry," he said wearily, "why do I work so hard at this? Notre Dame doesn't seem to care about my work for college basketball. Meeting after endless meeting trying to keep the game clean."

"You can't define yourself by what a few people seem to want."

"Yeah, but those few people control my life right now. They hold my whole career in their hands. What I'm doing out here on all these committees is worthless to them. What I've done in general is worthless; they see only what I haven't done."

I did my best to find consoling words, but he was right. The new plutocratic regime had different priorities. They measured success by the bottom line—money.

March drifted into April and April slouched toward May. Dick met with Malloy and Beauchamp, with the same results. "Father Malloy said," he told me after his final meeting, "that even if I won the national title next year, I was still finished coaching here."

"Did he say why?"

"Only that they want a change. I haven't done anything wrong; there are no negatives. Just that Notre Dame basketball had to be better in the 1990s."

"Better than what?"

"He didn't say."

"What did you tell him?"

"I told him that they would have to fire me. I'm not resigning."

2

D igger Phelps came striding toward me across the grass, bigger than life, with a huge cigar in his mouth, during a fall picnic at Rider College. I was a sophomore and the reigning homecoming queen (my brief stint with the crown-and-gown set) at the small college in New Jersey, and despite the fact that I had paraded around in a strapless gown with a tiara on my head for some of the past school year, I was a bit shy and extremely skeptical of guys who asked me for dates just because I was the homecoming queen. His presence filled the space around us, his brashness intimidated me, and I steeled myself to reject any advances from him. "I'm going to the Trenton State Fair tonight," he said with no introduction. "You want to go?"

I hesitated. If he had asked me for a date, I was ready to say no. But a fair? This didn't sound like he was asking me out. He disarmed me and jumped into my silence. "We met last year, remember?" he pressed. "At the basketball banquet." I wasn't much of a basketball fan and attended few games, but one of my queenly duties was to attend some sports banquets. He didn't play much and I didn't remember him as a player. But I *did* remember him from that banquet: sharply dressed and teasing me about my hat. "I'll pick you up at six. Don't eat, they have great hot dogs." He walked away. I was confused. Had I said yes?

Back at my sorority house, I ran into one of my sorority sisters who was a good friend of his. "What's Digger Phelps like?" I asked her.

"I think he's terrific," she said. "But let me tell you something about Digger Phelps. You love him or you hate him. There's nothing in between. Nobody's ever neutral about Digger Phelps."

Nor was I after that night at the fair (although he was wrong about the hot dogs). But our relationship was hindered by an unexpected obstacle: I hated the name Digger, a nickname he acquired as a kid because his father was an undertaker. The name had a hardness about it and seemed to embody his public exterior, a facade I had found to be quite thin. As a result, I avoided calling him anything for several months of dating. His family and friends in his hometown of Beacon, New York, called him "Richard," but I wasn't part of the family and felt uncomfortable using that name. I also felt uncomfortable with "Hey you." Finally, just before deciding to break off the relationship for lack of a name, I settled on the traditional nickname for Richard: "Dick."

We had dated for a few months when he asked me to do some typing for him. He actually typed better than I did, but those were the unenlightened days when guys asked girls to type for them and the girls said yes. I expected him to give me a handwritten draft of a course paper. Instead, he gave me letters beginning "Please consider this an application for a position on your basketball staff." He generously represented himself as a man for all seasons: "My chief aim is to coach young men of college age. I can also assist in baseball, golf, and other sports."

"So who's this Dean Smith and this Fordy Anderson?" I asked when I handed him the typed letters. "I thought you were going to be a funeral director like your father."

"I was. But last summer I worked on the playgrounds in Beacon and coached some of the high school kids for their summer league. I loved it. I want to try coaching so I'm applying for these jobs. How would you like being a coach's wife?" The next summer we were married. I still can't remember—did I say yes?

What I can remember from that time, with a quarter century of hindsight, is that I was unhappy at school, in the wrong major (pre-med), on scholarship and constantly out of money. I had become an indifferent student, drifting with no direction. By getting married, I acquired someone else's direction; I took on, as women did then, not only someone else's name, but his identity as well.

I also married because I wanted a family. My father had been killed in World War II and I had never known him. When I was three years old, I had been taken from my mother's relatives in England to a new and strange family, my father's, in Philadelphia. My mother remarried but was subsequently divorced from my stepfather. Our family was disrupted and unhappy, and I learned at an early age to hide my vulnerability by putting up a self-sufficient front that few people were able to penetrate. But I was tired of taking care of myself. More than anything, I wanted a family of my own. I wanted a place where I felt safe.

But why Digger Phelps? Despite the brashness, despite the tough and noisy exterior, and despite the fact that my own unhappy childhood had caused me to build a wall between myself and the rest of the world, I trusted him with my life. He ignored my "leave me alone" exterior and wouldn't let me brood or feel sorry for myself. When I complained that I was finding out that I didn't want to be a doctor but that I had no idea what I wanted to do, he lectured me. "You set your goals too far out," he said. "Make them smaller, closer, so that you achieve small goals one by one." Then he added a phrase that became one of his hallmarks in coaching: "You have to believe," the consummate motivator even then. He knew where *he* was going and he was content to have me tag along, adopting his goals as my own. He was disarming, unconventional, unpredictable, cocky. I could see how he rubbed people the wrong way. He had little use for pretense and even less use for the "right" people. If he liked you, you were his friend for life; if he didn't like you, you knew it. Born on the Fourth of July, his birthday inevitably celebrated with parties and fireworks, what can you expect? Bigger than life, you love him or you hate him. I loved him.

And I wanted to be a coach's wife. It would be fun, I thought, to go to games, to entertain players. I baked chocolate chip cookies for Dick's team at Junior High School No. 4 in Trenton that year. That's what it would be like to be a coach's wife. He would coach basketball, win most of the games, and set young men on the right path for life (or ready them for the Game of Life, something like that). I would go to all the games and bake chocolate chip cookies. We would be a team. I would be a great coach's wife.

3

D own the rabbit hole, through the looking glass, into the wonderland of sports. I wonder what that starry-eyed cookie baker would have done if she could have had the merest glimpse of the future? If she could have seen the unreal world of cats with treacherous grins, of knights and rulers who are only playing cards?

Dean Smith and all the other coaches were unimpressed by the brash and confident young man from Rider College and did not invite Dick to join their basketball staffs. Dick continued teaching in a Trenton junior high school and helped out with the Rider basketball team. Even then he was obsessed with coaching. We spent many nights at basketball games scouting future Rider opponents. I became adept at keeping shot charts and patient with his tendency to diagram plays at the dinner table: the salt shaker was Player X, the pepper set a pick, salt passed to the fork—score! Still, basketball existed on the fringes of my consciousness and I busied myself with school and sorority business. No one knew who

Digger Phelps was; no one cared about his lovelywife.

Then—through the invisible yet potent rumor mill of jobs for future coaches—in 1965 Dick heard about an opening for a basketball coach at a little Catholic high school in Hazleton, Pennsylvania. He and I climbed into our green Mustang convertible and drove into the coal region to talk to Father Ray Deviney and Father Joe Conboy, the priests at St. Gabriel's High School. They hired him on the spot. He was exactly what they were looking for: young, energetic, and willing to work for next to nothing. Now pregnant with our first child, I quit school and we moved to Hazleton, into a small, second-floor apartment, complete with sloping ceilings.

Although getting to college had been a driving force in my life, I was not unhappy about quitting school to follow Dick to his new job. First, back then, that was what women did. We didn't think about it—just packed up and went along. I was, of course, not unaffected by the predominant female stereotype of my formative years: woman as wife, mother, helpmate—the persistent image of 1950s television as depicted on "Leave It to Beaver" and "Father Knows Best." Second, he knew exactly what he wanted—to be a basketball coach. I, on the other hand, was adrift. It was easier for me to be a wife and mother than to figure out how to be something else: he gave me an identity—I was the coach's wife.

Our social life in Hazleton consisted of Father Deviney and his friends, Father Joe Conboy and Father Larry Homer, coming nearly every night to our apartment to smoke cigars and play poker. They adopted us as their local family and when I went into labor, they told the nurses they were my "uncles" to gain admission into the labor room to visit me. Any men in the labor room, let alone priests, were a strange sight in those pre-Lamaze days. We chatted between my contractions, and when I felt a labor pain coming, I politely apologized for interrupting the conversation with my groans.

Afterwards, sitting at our round oak kitchen table with Karen in my arms, I learned that a straight flush beats a full house and that Catholic priests (I was a recent convert) were not much like the stiff, teetotaling ministers of my Protestant childhood. My college roommate's mother, who lived in Hazleton, taught me to bake bread and make quilts. As I meticulously put the tiny stitches in a crib quilt I was making for Karen, I thought about how safe I felt, how Dick and I were going to build our life there. When Phil Sarno, a local sportswriter, wrote that Dick was overrated and had no future as a coach, I shrugged off the momentary sting. When a player's father accosted Dick on the steps of the church and accused him of being "prejudiced against Hungarians" because Dick had made his son leave practice to get a haircut, I dismissed it as an overreaction from a hypersensitive parent.

Even then Dick had Notre Dame on his mind. He called his team the "Irish" and asked me to figure out a way to put green shamrocks on the team uniforms. While preparing for the season, he wrote a letter to Notre Dame football coach Ara Parseghian. Not yet having begun his first official coaching job, he wrote: "Eventually, I'd like to coach on the college level. My big dream is to coach basketball at Notre Dame. I love the essence that makes Notre Dame what it is. Someday I hope that I might be part of that program." When he showed me the letter, I was not surprised. I had grown used to his quixotic aspirations. I did have some reservations, however, about his final paragraph: "Knowing that you have little time to waste, I don't expect you to answer the letter within the near future, but I would appreciate a short reply after the season, if your busy schedule permits."

"Don't you think that's a little pushy?" I asked.

He disagreed. "I said I know he's busy. I said he doesn't have to answer right away." A typewriter was beyond our modest means, so Dick hand-printed the letter and mailed it that afternoon. Meanwhile, I cut shamrocks out of green felt and sewed them on the team's purple-and-white uniforms: a questionable fashion statement but it worked its magic. Tiny St. Gabriel's High

School had eighteen boys in the senior class and four of them played on the basketball team. They ran hard, pressed full court, and won game after game. Even the school principal, Sister Davidica, who was cynical about the hoop hysteria that began to permeate her school, became a believer and led the nuns in a rosary before each game: "Just for good luck, Mr. Phelps," she said. When the St. Gabriel's "Irish" entered the state playoffs, Dick and Father Deviney drove six hours across Pennsylvania to scout St. Joe's of Williamsport, the primary obstacle on the way to the state championship. St. Gabriel's won five straight playoff games and the Class C State Championship. Crusty Monsignor Maher, the pastor of the church, wept at the news.

I can still see Petie O'Donnell, Ray McBrearty, and Eddie O'Donnell, three of the starting players, in our apartment after the championship game, Ray with a net around his neck, their arms around each other, celebrating the sweetness of victory. I sit in this mental picture, holding Karen and wanting the moment to last forever. A month later, Dick Harter, just having been appointed head coach at the University of Pennsylvania, called to ask Dick to be his assistant coach.

Dick took a cut in pay to move to the Penn job and I was pregnant with our second child. Baby-sitters were as far outside our budget as typewriters so when I attended games I took the toddling Karen along. She, not yet two years old, and I spent many nights in the Palestra, sitting through three games: the freshman game that Dick coached and a Big Five doubleheader. It was the heyday of Big Five basketball, in which Penn, St. Joseph, Villanova, Temple, and LaSalle competed for the mythical Big Five championship. The rivalries were intense and the Palestra, Penn's old gymnasium on campus, was jammed with students cheering on the teams and mocking the other schools. At twenty-two, I was scarcely older than the students and found myself caught up in the Palestra spirit. If Penn did well, I was thrilled. If not, that was the head coach's problem.

Other nights, far more numerous, I spent at home alone as Dick developed a reputation as a masterful recruiter. In those pre-NCAA regulation days, a coach could see a high school player as frequently as he liked, and for a school like Penn, perennially at the bottom of the Ivy League and the Big Five, the recruiting efforts had to be intense. In addition, Penn, as an Ivy League school, did not give athletic scholarships. All financial aid was based, for athletes as for all students, on need. A recruiter's goal was to get in as many applications as possible and to spend days, weeks perhaps, with the top prospects. At seventeen or eighteen years old, a prospective player could easily be flattered by constant attention from some slickly dressed young assistant coach.

Although I played a small part by helping to entertain re-cruits when they came to Penn's campus for a visit, I was clearly outside the action. Dick and Dick Harter picked up the recruits at the Philadelphia airport, distracted them with conversation as they drove by the grim wasteland of oil storage tanks that lined the highway between the airport and Penn's campus, and cautiously chose the least littered routes around Penn's inner-city campus for the official tour. Once Dick even dashed ahead of Dick Harter and a recruit to pick up blowing newspapers as Dick Harter explained the benefits of an urban campus to the recruit from Ohio. My presence at recruiting dinners actually mattered little, but they provided a way to get a restaurant meal. And they allowed me a little time with my husband, who now spent more time in airports and hotels than he did at home.

I spent most of my time counting the hours until Dick would be home, watching Penn games on the local television station, pushing Karen in her stroller for hours and hours around our apartment complex, and visiting the local public library to ex-change the books that kept me company. I read voraciously and indiscriminately: Hemingway, Fitzgerald, Cather, Sayers, and Christie replaced the Nancy Drew books that had filled up my lonely childhood. It was clear that the Penn program did not need me: not to bake chocolate chip cookies, not to type letters, not to sew shamrocks on uniforms.

Dick went out and sold Penn and he did it well. After four years of his recruiting, Penn was winning both the Ivy League and the Big Five. Dick coached the Penn freshman to the first undefeated season in forty years; "You have to believe" was posted in the freshman locker room. Penn was fast becoming a national power. Dick was on his way.

4

n my Law and Literature class in the law school, my students were discussing *The Death of Ivan Ilych* and *To Kill a Mockingbird*. We began the semester by reading Plato, focusing first on the duty to obey the law—especially if the law is wrong. As the semester neared its end, my seminar of third-year law students read these novels by Leo Tolstoy and Harper Lee as part of a section on the professional lives of lawyers. They struggled with the books, peering through them at their own futures. Ivan Ilych, a lawyer, did everything according to form. He married an appropriate woman, made the proper job advances: "on the whole his life ran its course as he believed life should do; easily, pleasantly, decorously." Yet he died a painful, lonely death bereft of any love except that of a servant he despised. For the sake of appearances, he had alienated all those who might have loved him.

Ilych stands in sharp contrast to Atticus Finch, the lawyer in *To Kill a Mockingbird*, who defied his community by representing the black Tom Robinson against a trumped-up rape charge. Atticus fully knew that the jury in Maycomb, Alabama would convict, yet he stayed true to his course, trusting that his community would recognize the truth about itself even if it could not act in accordance with that truth. Atticus didn't worry about appearances; this is how he differed crucially from Ivan Ilych. He stood up for the truth even when the truth was unpopular. He believed that in the "secret courts of men's hearts," he was vindicated and the truth was known.

In class I made it simple. "Remember what Plato said about the truth: 'We must not think so much what the many say of us; we must think of what truth herself will say of us.' " My students would have choices to make in their lives as lawyers and perhaps something we discovered together in these books would help them. One chooses the truth, of course; what could be more fundamental?

"It's simple," I said to Dick afterwards over lunch at the Cornucopia Restaurant in downtown South Bend. He picked me up at the law school right after my class and the classroom discussion had not left my mind. "They're asking you to lie. I don't care how they paint it. They want you to say you're resigning, that you *want* to resign, when you're actually being fired." Dick flinched visibly at the word "fired," and I was momentarily sorry that I had been so blunt. I reached out and took his hand across the table. "Look, I'm sorry. But I can't stand in front of the classroom and talk about the importance of truth and watch this happen. The hypocrisy is too much for me. I feel like I'm drowning in it!"

Dick pulled his hand away and gestured impatiently, nearly knocking over his mug of Yogi tea, his favorite, a blend of strong black tea, milk, and cardamom seed. His gestures are always wide and his body moves along with his hands and arms. He uses his hands, moving them from side to side, to fill the spaces as he searches for words.

"You're drowning! How do you think I feel? After nineteen years my job description has changed. I'm to fill the seats, no matter what. And there's nothing I can do. I'm dumped on the whim of a new administration. You know how it works around here." Indeed I did. Father Hesburgh, who was the University president for thirty-five years, had recently retired and been replaced. According to the University charter, any Notre Dame president must be a priest from the Indiana Province of the Holy Cross Order. The pool of qualified and experienced candidates is small. Despite this, the structure of governance at Notre Dame puts all power in the hands of the president and whomever he chooses to delegate power. Once it has selected the president, the board of trustees acts only in an advisory capacity and the faculty has virtually no voice at all. The monolithic organization of university governance is a perennial sore point among the faculty but it never seems to change. The extreme hierarchy is an unusual way to run things, but it does mirror the governance of the Catholic Church and of many religious orders. Notre Dame is very "Catholic" in the way it distributes decision-making.

"I've been arguing for years that university presidents should be in control of their athletic departments. Presidents should be involved so that a program is clean—no NCAA violations and a reasonable percentage of the athletes graduating." Dick's egg salad sandwich arrived and he stopped talking to turn his attention to it.

"And yours is perfect in those areas." I picked at my malfatti. We'd been eating at the Cornucopia since it opened fifteen years ago, and I always ordered malfatti. No imagination.

"Right. That's the irony. I'm not sure that presidents involved with won–lost percentages is a great idea."

"Didn't Father Hesburgh once tell you that you could stay at Notre Dame as long as you wanted?"

"Uh-huh. A promise not worth the paper it isn't written on now that he's no longer president."

"So you're learning something about contract law, are you?" I waggled my fingers at Father John Dunne, a friend of ours who was sitting alone across the way. John, a Holy Cross priest and a Notre Dame theology professor, has written books that have inspired me. He writes of the personal journey to God, of the need for solitude and reflection. A quiet and gentle man, his classes are always oversubscribed; the students adore him. "You know, I've always envied John Dunne. His life is so peaceful, so contemplative. There's a part of me that could have been a cloistered nun."

"A very small part, Terry. *Very* small." Dick made a check-writing gesture in the waitress's direction. Dick and I met John Dunne through our friends Jim and Mary Ann Roemer, who brought many Notre Dame people into our lives. We met Jim and Mary Ann, the first non-sports people who became our close friends, at a dinner party when Jim was practicing law in South Bend and was part-time counsel for the University, nearly twenty years ago. Jim had recently given up a lucrative position with Lockheed on the West Coast to return to South Bend, his hometown. Jim is second-generation Notre Dame; his father taught philosophy at the University and he was raised just a block away from where we now live, a stone's throw from the campus. He and Mary Ann had become disenchanted with the fast and superficial California lifestyle and had come home.

Shortly after that dinner party, Mary Ann called to ask me if I wanted to go to a class with her, one taught by a legendary Notre Dame English professor, Frank O'Malley. Mary Ann's five children were all in their teens, nearly grown up, and Mary Ann was auditing classes. "O'Malley is very important to me," Mary Ann said as we walked across the south quad to the classroom. "I wrote a paper for him that he liked so much that he read it to the class. It was a short story really. It started with how I like to walk down streets at night, looking into the lighted windows of houses and imagining the love and warmth inside. Then I wrote about my own childhood and how hard it was."

"How?" I was entranced by this strong yet soft woman who so easily opened up to me.

"My mother died when I was ten. My father couldn't handle it, not her sickness or her death. Or raising me without her. So I went to live with relatives with one of my brothers. But then he was killed in a sledding accident. My aunt and uncle were kind to me but it seemed that I kept losing people that I dared to love."

"You talk about all that so easily. My own childhood was pretty messed up but I can't talk about it. I don't even like to think about it."

"I used to be like that, to be tough, to protect myself from getting hurt again. Yet once you have children, you're vulnerable. If you don't open yourself up, you can't be much of a mother, or a friend, or anything. All you are is safe."

Frank O'Malley was well past his prime when I finally went to his class that day. He was one of the last of the Notre Dame "dons," who never married, lived in the dorm with his boys, and made the University his life. In his day, he was a brilliant teacher and had legions of devoted former students and protégés. But he never really let anyone get close to him. Instead he took to drink and it was beginning to show, even in a morning class. But that day it wasn't Frank O'Malley whose words changed my life. It was Mary Ann with her sure but gentle, "All you are is safe."

Mary Ann transcended a rocky childhood and became a loving and open woman who taught me that one of the paradoxes of life is that true power comes from being vulnerable. The tough little girl I had been who never dared to let people come close melted in the warmth of her personality and her friendship. She was foster mother, big sister, best friend. Jim and Mary Ann introduced us to the social concern side of the University, as they were involved in everything from the Holy Cross Associates (a year of volunteer work after graduation) to Neighborhood Study Help (students tutoring children in the South Bend community). They pulled us outside ourselves, made us aware of others, and, perhaps most important, stirred our interest in working with the less fortunate, an interest that Dick and I found we deeply shared with each other.

Predictably enough, even at this our styles differed. I tended to be up close, personal, and, as always, private; Dick was flashy and flamboyant. Mary Ann talked me into all sorts of things. She asked me to host a "Senior Reflection Group," a gathering of about a dozen Notre Dame seniors at our house once a month. The students took turns cooking dinner and selecting a topic for discussion. The students were content to let me hover in the background; they grew accustomed to my being quiet, offering an occasional observation, or spurring on their discussion with a question. Because of Dick's travel schedule, he was rarely present. But when he was, the ambiance changed dramatically. The students' attention was riveted on him. He held the floor (pontificated, to my mind); he filled the room and the students left ready to change the world.

Influenced by Mary Ann and her work, I quietly became involved in law school social justice programs when I started work there. In 1980, my first year on the law faculty, some students asked me to accompany them on the first GALILEE program. During this GALILEE, an acronym for Group Alternative Live-In Legal Education, I lived for three days with Mrs. Ramirez and her son, Juan, in a section of South Chicago called "Little Village." The other four students lodged in other homes in the neighborhood and each day we visited places in which the legal needs of the poor arose and places that served these needs: Cook County Jail, violence court, soup kitchens and shelters, the Legal Aid Bureau, and legal services storefront offices. I became the adviser to GALILEE and now each year about fifty law students, often with me along as a participant, spend three days over their semester break living in the inner cities—New York, Los Angeles, Detroit, Washington, D.C., Boston, Cincinnati, and Houston have joined the list—learning about the legal needs of the urban poor.

Dick tended more toward the grand gesture. To be fair, he occasionally got his hands dirty (quite literally the Christmas day that he and Jim Roemer scrubbed toilets at the Center for the Homeless). But he learned to combine the glad-handing, crowd-wooing part of himself with his desire to make a difference. In 1982, eighteen of his former players returned to Notre Dame, ten of whom were in the NBA, to play a game for Dick's favorite charity, Logan Center. Bill Laimbeer, Kelly Tripucka, Orlando Woolridge, Adrian Dantley, Bill Hanzlik, and the others pulled on blue or gold scrimmage shirts one more time and played all-out in front of a capacity crowd. Logan Center was $50,000 happier for their efforts. Thanks to Jim and Mary Ann, thanks to Notre Dame, we both learned to find the best parts of ourselves and give a little back.

Despite nineteen years of Notre Dame and our close friendship with Jim and Mary Ann, we were reluctant to confide even in them because of the secrecy surrounding Dick's requested resignation. In private, Dick and I discussed the "topic" endlessly and it drew us together and drove us apart. I was reminded of a powerful dance sequence in Zeffirelli's *Romeo and Juliet,* in which the star-crossed lovers dance toward each other palms outward and away from each other palms inward, an image of simultaneous attraction and repulsion. We danced likewise, becoming each other's best and only friend and confidant. Yet I reached points when I said, calmly at first, "Let's not talk about it anymore." And then, clenching my teeth and eventually screaming, "I can't stand talking about this!" I knew I was not being fair, that I encouraged his talking to me. I felt his pain and bewilderment and I wanted to make it go away. I began to wonder if we would survive this.

The big chill that descended on us at Notre Dame had been foreshadowed by signs of frost for quite some time: small omens, but in retrospect clear indicators that the new administration, now in its third year, did not hold us in much esteem. Little things like the new University president, Father Malloy, not bothering to respond to the invitation to our older daughter Karen's wedding, although Karen, while attending Notre Dame, had been a student in his theology class; or the fact that we had never been invited to

Dick Rosenthal's house after he became athletic director. This was particularly strange because the Rosenthals had been our friends. When Dick Rosenthal was a bank president, we had stayed in the Rosenthals' condominium in Vail. My husband had even learned to ski on Rosenthals' skis. The recent slights were trivial, but significant.

The year was difficult in other ways as well. The schedule, which Rosenthal had taken over from Dick, was brutal. I had never seen a team so tired. As a rule, coaches control their own non-conference schedules and pad them generously with games designed to build confidence and accumulate "W's." Schedules should be variable enough to allow players some respite, not to mention some rest and a chance to be real students, if only for a few days. Dick was particularly adamant about not playing over exams. All that changed and he wrote memos in vain; no one listened. His years of success meant nothing.

There was something ominous in the air, almost a feeling of sabotage. Everything Dick wanted to do to improve the program was vetoed. He thought the dominance of conferences had cut deeply into his recruiting and requested that we look into joining a conference. The young Big East Conference in particular had eroded much of Dick's recruiting base. He had had a solid pipeline to many eastern cities, such as New York and Washington, D.C. Now, however, kids in those places grew up on a steady diet of Big East hype in the media. Seton Hall, Boston College, and Connecticut—relatively unknown before—had become popular, much-televised basketball schools, and they were closer to home for the kids in those cities, prone to homesickness before they even left. The formation of the Big East Conference had worked its magic. Not that joining the Big East was the answer for us in the heartland of the Midwest, but the day of powerful independents was over. The other independents— Marquette, Dayton, DePaul—had seen the writing on the wall and joined conferences. The answer from Notre Dame was

"Sorry, no." Notre Dame didn't need to be in a conference.

Then during the year there was the fracas over the "Hoops for the Homeless" game. Dick got involved in this project, in which part of the proceeds of a nationally televised basketball game would go to the Center for the Homeless in South Bend. Sonny Vaccaro, a familiar face in basketball circles as the Nike representative responsible for its summer basketball camps, came to Dick with the concept of using college sports to raise money for the homeless. Vaccaro suggested that the Notre Dame–LSU game in New Orleans would be a good matchup to launch the project, which would then recur each year with different schools. This year it would result in $50,000 going to the shelter in South Bend. The shelter was particularly important to us: two of our close friends, D'Arcy Chisholm and Dave Link, had founded it.

Dick thought the charity game was a natural for Notre Dame and that Notre Dame was a natural for it. In fact, he was pleased that Notre Dame was asked to initiate the game, that Notre Dame was seen as a leader in utilizing sports for the larger good. He had erred by assuming that everyone would agree with him. The athletic director was irate that he was brought into the project too late to refuse, writing Dick that Notre Dame's "rechanneling contributions [the ticket and television revenue, I suppose] is a questionable right, and our willingness to participate in this one event is by no means a suggestion that we would entertain such proposals from any other charity, no matter how worthy."

And a few weeks later when the team returned to campus after a last-second victory over Syracuse in the Carrier Dome, a few hundred students met the bus and the players and coaches spilled out to greet the crowd. Dick Rosenthal, who had accompanied the team, sat inside the bus with his head buried in a book, apparently less than elated at the students' enthusiasm. It was becoming increasingly clear, visible even, that Dick and the new athletic director had some very basic philosophical differences about the role of athletics in the University and in society.

Despite all this we had until recently felt secure. Even if the new administration wanted to sweep us out with its new broom, hey, this was Notre Dame. Even if some students and local fans were infected by the "win-at-any-cost" fever, this *was* Notre Dame. At Notre Dame, as I always bragged to other coaches' wives, a coach was simply not subject to the vicissitudes of public opinion. Alumni, fans, boosters, whatever, had no influence on whether a coach kept his job or not. "A coach has only to please two men—Father Hesburgh (the University president) and Father Joyce (the executive vice-president, in charge of the athletic program)—and what they want is a competitive program that treats the players like students and wins enough games without breaking any rules," I would say smugly. And those men, priests, could not be seduced by wealthy alumni or boosters or television money. Surely a change in administration could never mean the end of a coach's career. Even if the new University and athletic department administrators would have preferred their own man as head basketball coach, one whose national reputation in education and athletics did not eclipse their own, Notre Dame did not dispose of people who had served it well.

Comforted by this knowledge, I could be myself and had stopped worrying about whether I was an appropriate "coach's wife." I enrolled as a transfer student at Notre Dame in 1972—the first year women were admitted. I graduated among the first 150 female "domers," Notre Dame women graduates. Our lives became greatly involved in the life of the University, and along the way I earned two more Notre Dame degrees (I am still, I think, the only female "triple domer") and took a position on the law school faculty. Our friends were deans, priests, counselors, poets, rectors, mechanics—all Notre Dame people. My students mixed with Dick's players regularly at gatherings at our house. We believed in, we lived, the rhetoric of the "Notre Dame family."

Like politics, coaching involves the family. What a coach does is of intense public interest and if he blunders, the kids in elementary school know about it and they usually taunt the coach's children with their knowledge. A coach works in public, literally before thousands, and his family is usually present. It was challenging raising children in the fishbowl of Notre Dame basketball, and the forced public nature of our lives in some ways made us acutely private and inspired a family loyalty that might have bordered on the fanatical. It fostered a kind of addiction to privacy, to the shelter of a closed family unit as the only space not subject to public scrutiny. But also, we felt sheltered by what we actually experienced as the "Notre Dame family"—people in charge at Notre Dame who made us feel we belonged there, that we were part of a mission, part of a vision of a great university.

When the boos began, then, family support became critical. But the larger solution seemed simple to me. All the University officials had to do was make a public statement of support: "This is our coach. We all support him." Or words to that effect. If they preferred symbolism to words, Father Malloy or Father Beauchamp could be the team chaplain for a game and even sit on the bench. Father Hesburgh had always acted as team chaplain at least once a season, saying Mass for the team before the game and sitting on the bench during the game. Father Hesburgh did not hover around Notre Dame sports and disliked Notre Dame being too quickly identified as a sports power. Local legend has it that when Father Hesburgh became president of the University in the fifties, he saw its football prowess and fame as interfering with his academic aspirations for Notre Dame. He toyed with the idea of deemphasizing football, but soon discovered that football was too much a part of the fabric of the place. There are still those who believe that football gets in the way of Notre Dame becoming a great academic institution: that if we were less concerned with our ranking in football and more concerned with our ranking among schools with Nobel Prizes won by faculty and alumni, we'd be better off. But even those cynics acknowledge, albeit begrudgingly, that without football Notre Dame might well be "St. Mary's of the Cornfields" when it comes to national recognition. Yet it makes for some tension and many of Notre Dame's excellent faculty bristle when people invariably say, "Oh yes, Notre Dame. You have that great football team."

The direct control of the athletic department was the charge of the executive vice-president, Father Joyce, but no one doubted that Father Hesburgh would have stepped in immediately if a sports program got out of hand or if a coach violated any rules. In many ways Father Hesburgh exemplified the kind of control of athletics that the NCAA was newly advocating. The NCAA's theory is that if college presidents pay attention to what's going on in their athletic programs and control their coaches, college sports will be cleaned up. So although Father Hesburgh generally kept his distance, he was definitely in charge and had an unerring sense of the importance of symbolic acts. It was important to all of us associated with sports, especially the team members, that Father Hesburgh recognize the efforts of a team as one of the aspects of a well-rounded university. Thus, once a year he, like many of the other priests on campus, was chaplain for a game. He was charmingly boastful of his personal won–loss record and his presence on the bench for notable upsets of number-one teams. I suspect he preferred these upsets to a number-one ranking—"giant-killers" rather than giants. Now a similar modest gesture, the new president or executive vice-president being chaplain for a game, would publicly demonstrate University support, silence the critics, and spare my family needless pain.

Plenty of sustenance came from outside the Notre Dame community: friends around the country wrote encouraging letters; Reebok ran a full-page advertisement in *USA Today* saying "We congratulate Digger Phelps on 400 wins and 50 victories," referring respectively to the number of games he had won and to players who had played four years for him who had graduated— all 50. In addition, the national press was generally favorable to the Notre Dame basketball program, despite the fact that Notre

Dame became a favorite whipping boy when it left the College Football Association television contract and privately contracted with NBC for televising Notre Dame football games. And plenty of support came privately from our friends at Notre Dame. But from the official Notre Dame, nothing but silence. I waited in vain for some sign of support. I began to feel that we had been thrown to the mob, disposed of like pieces of Notre Dame's debris. Many of the local sportswriters, largely in the University administration's pocket, jumped on the Digger-bashing bandwagon. Dick's eccentricities became major faults and the subject of constant local conversation.

In desperation, I talked to a couple of my trusted friends. One in particular had counseled me for years when I felt in conflict with the University; whether I was upset over general policy decisions or personal job problems, he always gave me good advice. He is a wise and generous-spirited man, who knows how to play University politics like a pro. Early in my career, my unmitigated impulses would have led me to storm into offices or fire off irate memos. (And become, as Dick once put it, a "superficial lamb.") Luckily, I always turned to my friend for advice first. "Don't go down in the burning plane," he usually says. He has taught me to hold my tongue and bide my time. He has schooled me in diplomacy and compromise.

But now both my other confidant and he said, "Make them fire him." They were as stunned as we were and when they asked what the reasons were, I could not provide an answer. No one mentioned a burning plane.

I'm a fighter pilot's daughter. My father was one of the Americans who joined the Royal Canadian Air Force before the United States entered World War II. As a child, I fantasized that he joined up on principle, that he saw what was occurring in Europe and wanted to fight it. That might be true. What is probably truer, though, is that he wanted to fly. He got his wish and flew a Spitfire on missions out of England until his plane went down in the Bay of Biscay in 1943, eight months before I was born.

My first year of life in England was the last year of the war. I have no conscious memories of it, of course, just as I have no memories of my father. But I'm like him, everyone says, a fighter pilot's daughter: I have his spirit and I felt it intensely. The desire to fight what I perceived as injustice was strong; it was also foolhardy and perhaps pointless.

When I tried to pray, my words stuck in my throat. I felt like Huck Finn when he tried to pray for the strength to return Jim to slavery—"You can't pray a lie. I found that out," he said. My already fragile health deteriorated: my vision blurred and I stumbled when I walked. I knew these chronic problems were intensified by stress, but I could not relax. Some days I thought I would go crazy.

My dreams were filled with images of disaster and violence. One night I dreamed that I was accused of a crime, of being crazy, and the authorities planned to commit me to an institution. If I protested or got angry, my emotional behavior supported their point, so I didn't know how to act. At a banquet I made a speech about what was happening to me but I could tell that everyone, including Dick, thought my speaking out was inappropriate. I awakened, very frightened.

I wondered why I felt so agonized. The constant hype over sports at Notre Dame had long since quenched the sports fan in me; the thought of never having to go to another Notre Dame game actually pleased me. The fact that my days as a coach's wife were numbered made me happy, not sad. I thought that Dick had outgrown coaching years before and urged him to quit. Besides, he wasn't going to coach forever. He was planning to get out in the next few years anyway. So, what was obsessing me?

Some years ago, Marie Louise von Franz, the renowned Jungian psychologist, spoke at a conference at Notre Dame. I had coffee with her and told her about one of my dreams. In the dream

I had a magic necklace which had the power to make me invisible. I entrusted the necklace to someone who used it to hurt me. "Why do you feel so much pain?" von Franz asked.

"Because I was betrayed. I risked becoming visible, risked letting the world see what I stood for. I trusted and I was betrayed."

"But isn't it better to be betrayed than to be the betrayer?"

Her words returned to me, and I repeated them over and over like a litany. Was that it? Did I feel betrayed? Whatever it was, it extended far beyond any coaching job. Like a reluctant lover, who once smitten is unable to believe the beloved has flaws, I fell hard for the Notre Dame myth, the vision of family, of caring and compassion. Was that vision a fraud? Had I been taken in, betrayed? It infected the air we breathed, it tainted the food we ate. And always hanging over us in neon lights was a single word: "Why?"

5

Lay 1990 came reluctantly to South Bend. Outside our house the dogwood buds finally exploded into blossom, and their cruciform blooms curtained our bedroom windows. How much these trees had grown since we bought this house nineteen years ago! When we first visited South Bend in May 1971 for the press conference at which Dick was announced as the new head basketball coach, I found this old, brick house in the "faculty ghetto," less than a mile from the campus. I spent the day looking at houses with Agnes Bartholomew, a real estate saleswoman and the wife of a Notre Dame professor. The Bartholomews had lived in the neighborhood for nearly thirty years. "We've seen a lot of coaches come and go," she told me over lunch.

Not us, I thought. We had moved seven times in six years, leaving behind two newly built houses in New Jersey and New York as Dick moved up the coaching ladder. As far as we were concerned, this was our last move. We did not intend to leave our Indiana home in a hurry.

After looking at a dozen houses with Agnes, I narrowed the lot to three. The next day Dick went with me and together we chose this one. *"This* is the kind of house our children should grow up in," Dick said the minute he walked through the door. He was right. It was exactly the way we had dreamed of living in a college town. We could walk to the campus; Dick could come home for lunch. Moose Krause, the athletic director, lived down the street, as did the sports information director, Roger Valdiserri. Notre Dame faculty lived all around us. A big, old brick house with lots of room for children, books, students, all the things we dreamed would fill it during our years there.

We were advised that the house was not a particularly good investment, that it was more financially prudent to buy into one of the new developments expanding the town to the east and the north. It wasn't until years later that I discovered that the house was an excellent example of "Prairie Renaissance" architecture, a midwestern style influenced by Frank Lloyd Wright. But in 1971 we did not see this house as an investment. This *was* the place where my children should grow up. I earnestly hoped that they could, that the vagabond nature of a coach's life was over for us. We were home at last.

This is not to say that I came eagerly to South Bend, Indiana. Since I left England at the age of three, I had spent my entire life on the East Coast. I had never been west of Philadelphia and, like so many easterners, I did not think traveling west of Philadelphia was necessary for the good life. Although we moved around as Dick graduated from being a high school coach to an assistant college coach to a head coach, his jobs were in the East: Trenton, New Jersey; Hazleton, Pennsylvania; Philadelphia; the Bronx. A comedian's list of cities no one wants to visit.

But Dick had written that fateful letter to Ara Parseghian. Completely undeterred by Parseghian's fame or the fact that no one, especially Parseghian, had ever heard of Digger Phelps, Dick wrote that he loved Notre Dame and he wanted to be basketball coach at Notre Dame someday. When, to everyone's surprise but his, Dick actually *became* head basketball coach at Notre Dame, Ara dug Dick's hand-written note, which he had never answered, out of his "crazy letter" file. Roger Valdiserri distributed copies to the press, which printed it widely, enamored of Dick's dream-come-true story.

But Dick's much-publicized dream to coach at Notre Dame was *his* dream, not mine. I had been raised neither Catholic nor Irish and Notre Dame was not my mecca as it seemed to be for most American Catholics. Where I grew up, the Ivy League was considered the place to go to school. When the many job offers descended on Dick after his wonder year at Fordham, the position I favored was at the University of Pennsylvania, the school of choice in the Waspy Philadelphia suburb where I had been raised. Dick had been an assistant at Penn for four years; we knew our way around and were comfortable there. For all I knew about the Midwest, Indiana had only recently joined the Union. And all I knew about Notre Dame was centered on Father Hesburgh's civil rights work and that Ara Parseghian was the best-looking football coach in the country.

But Dick was another story. He was raised by an Irish Catholic mother; Notre Dame was as much a part of his childhood as being an altar boy, attending CYO dances, and standing in line each Saturday for confession. On Saturdays in the fall he lay across his boyhood bed with his ear pressed to the radio as he listened to Notre Dame football games. And after the games, when the neighborhood boys played their own version in the street outside, Dick's opponents could be any *other* team they wanted: *he* played for Notre Dame. For many American Catholics, Notre Dame football's perennial superiority compensated for the daily slights in the workplace and in society that were directed at newly arrived immigrants: "No Catholics Allowed," "No Irish Need Apply." For two or three blissful hours on Saturday afternoon, all that was obliterated. Notre Dame football represented who they could be, who they *would* be. On Saturday afternoons the Catholics weren't just as good as everybody else—they were *better*. Never mind that Knute Rockne wasn't Catholic or even many of the players; the very name of the place—Notre Dame— "Our Lady"—well, it was like starting to pray.

Overt prejudice toward Catholics had nearly evaporated by Dick's boyhood in the late forties, but the magic remained. Even after Dick and I were married, phrases like "Hanratty to Seymour! Touchdown!" were as much a part of our weekend ritual as the Latin phrases we murmured while attending Mass. So I hadn't even bothered to voice my dissent; for Dick, there *was* no other school. He was destined for Notre Dame.

The day before the press conference, Dick and I drove from our home in Beacon, New York, to LaGuardia Airport to fly to South Bend. When Dick had become the head basketball coach at Fordham, we built a little Cape Cod house on a pond in Beacon, New York, Dick's hometown. We moved in a few days before Christmas and just when I had finally unpacked the last box and hung the last curtain, John Dee announced that he was leaving as the Notre Dame basketball coach. A few days later it was clear that we were moving to South Bend.

We stopped on our way to LaGuardia at Fordham where Dick met with the team to tell them that he was leaving. As I waited, I walked around the Rosehill campus, touching the bricks of the buildings, tearful with nostalgia for a place where we had only spent one year. I had been able to return to school at Fordham and was happily working toward my abandoned-for-marriage undergraduate degree. The basketball season had been successful and fun, and I had come to love this campus in the heart of the Bronx. I was even beginning to feel like a New Yorker.

Two days at Notre Dame changed all that and I returned to New York a converted Notre Dame fan—not of the sports program, but of the place itself. In those two days I found a house I loved just walking distance from the campus. The campus: the

Golden Dome, the Grotto, the light bricks of the classroom buildings and dormitories, all aglow in the spring sunlight, the tulip
trees which dotted the campus just beginning to bud. We had had
dinner with Roger and Elaine Valdiserri and Eleanor VanderHa-
gen, Moose Krause's secretary, and her husband. They were
Notre Dame through and through. We had lingered over lunch at
the Morris Inn with Father Joyce, the executive vice-president
who had hired Dick. The bustle and tension of the East Coast
were absent. A different quality of life emanated from the heartland and from Notre Dame.

Still it took me all summer to pack. I couldn't complain in the
light of Dick's palpable delight in getting the job of his dreams. He
promptly disappeared to take up any unfinished recruiting and to
participate in Notre Dame golf tournaments.

"I know it's tough on you, leaving you here to pack up again,
but it's part of the job and I have to do it," he told me.

I managed to keep a straight face. "I understand. *Somebody*
has to play in those charity golf tournaments with Ara Parseghian
and Andy Williams and—who else? Don't worry about me. I'll
just stay at home and teach the children to sing the Fight Song."

The children learned the Fight Song, lisping out "Cheer,
cheer for old Notre Dame" all summer to anyone who would
listen. Our belongings disappeared once again into the boxes that
I hadn't yet had time to throw away. In early August our furniture
and the little sailboat that I sailed on our pond were hauled into
the moving van. We piled into our station wagon—two adults,
three children, two dogs—and set out for Indiana. I felt like a
pioneer woman in her covered wagon as I watched the cornfields
unfold along Route 80. We were young, excited, optimistic.

That first year challenged my optimism and confirmed my
secret fears. The team went 6 and 20, along the way suffering a
humiliating 65-point loss to our old buddy Bobby Knight at Indiana. Dick and Bobby had been friendly rivals for years. They
became friends when Bobby coached at West Point, just across the

Hudson River from Dick's hometown, Beacon. When Dick became a head coach, his Fordham team beat Bobby's cadets. Then, both twenty-nine years old, they landed in the same state in the Midwest, the youngest head coaches in the country.

In their first intrastate meeting, Bobby held a decided advantage. Despite appearances, he *wasn't* running up the score; even his substitutes never missed and our players just couldn't hit. Late in the game, Bobby looked down the bench at Dick and shrugged, helpless in reducing the embarrassing spread. Our team was so bad that Adolph Rupp, Kentucky's coach, called Dick's room after Notre Dame had lost to Kentucky by a mere 18, wondering what he had done wrong that the score was so close. Roger Valdiserri, blessed with a sense of humor to match his keen intellect, dubbed the hapless team "The Gang That Couldn't Shoot Straight."

The only thing worse than the team was the South Bend winter as the temperatures plunged to well below zero, with wind chills (my introduction to the protean beauty of Lake Michigan) in minus double digits. For the first time in my life, I saw ice form on the insides of windows.

But even losses and bitter weather could not squelch our enthusiasm for the kind of life we hoped to build there. Dick was determined that we all would come to love Notre Dame as he did. When our four-year-old, Ricky, moped around because he had left his best friend in New York, Dick took him by the hand and the two of them went down our street, door-to-door, "looking for boys." "You can't imagine how peculiar they looked," our neighbor Mary Lou Derwent told me later. "This big guy and a little boy at my door asking if we had any boys! It did give me pause. But they knew they'd hit the jackpot at my house when I told them that I had *four* boys."

We had hit the jackpot. We were welcomed into the neighborhood with parties and casseroles and bottles of wine. In lovely midwestern sunsets, I walked the children to the campus past the cemetery to the lakes to feed the ducks. "Is this heaven?" Rick asked one evening as we walked past the cemetery on our way home. Thinking he meant Notre Dame, I replied, "Sort of. Why do you ask?"

He pointed to the cemetery. "Because you told us people go to heaven when they die. And that's where people go when they die, so it must be heaven."

Dick's Fordham assistant, Frank McLaughlin, came with us to Notre Dame and so did Dick DiBiaso, an old friend who was an assistant at the University of Virginia. Dick DiBiaso's wife, Shawna, and I leaned heavily on each other and suffered through away games together. I took Karen, Rick, and Jenny to her house to play with Brian and Shawna-Re. Shawna and I would pool our dinners, tune in to the game, and commiserate as the team lost yet again, sharing a bottle of wine (and once, to our morning-after dismay, nearly a whole bottle of Harvey's Bristol Cream sherry, pouring it into Shawna's little crystal glasses and nervously slurping it all down).

Shawna was much more outgoing than I, and I trailed along in her wake, like a reluctant dinghy being pulled against the current, trying to make friends. In many ways, our roles were ironically reversed. Shawna would have been much better at being the head coach's wife, and I would have hidden contentedly in her shadow. She was sure of herself, open, friendly, the type you want at your party because she can talk to anybody. There was considerable collegiality in the athletic department at that time. There were parties, dinners, baby showers, coffee klatches for the wives. The gracious Elaine Valdiserri, whose husband Roger had come to Notre Dame as a student, took Shawna and me under her wing, trying to make sure we weren't neglected by the other wives. Sometimes, though, I felt uncomfortable and a little out-of-place. It was difficult for me to sort out who, of all the people who so eagerly welcomed us to Notre Dame, would have wanted to be our friends if Dick weren't the basketball coach. This confusion made me reluctant to share my private thoughts, my insecurities. I put on my happy, bland, Digger's wife face and went through the motions.

Because Dick and I were so much younger than the other head coaches—the age of most of the assistant coaches, in fact—it was among the assistant coaches and their wives that we seemed to have a natural fit. But that could be complicated. During that first year, Shawna and Dick DiBiaso were invited to an assistant football coach's house for a dinner party—fondue was the fashion then. When Shawna told me about it, I asked, rather hurt, why we hadn't been invited. This was our crowd, I had thought. We were usually invited to these gatherings. "Well, it was just assistant coaches," Shawna explained.

"So? I don't see what difference that makes, we're all friends, aren't we?"

"Yes, but . . . assistant coaches are a little distrustful of head coaches. They like to get together and complain about their bosses. Digger is a 'boss,' Terry. You guys don't always fit in."

Where did we fit in? We were the age of the assistants but not their peers. The townspeople who were used to socializing with the head coaches tended to be a generation ahead of us: we were the age of their children. Although they were polite to us, nice in their way, we weren't going to step comfortably into their social circle. I knew how easily coaches fell out of favor and were deserted by their "friends." Years later the "Gerry Faust phenomenon" made me more aware of the mercurial popularity of coaches. Gerry and Marlene Faust arrived in town to unprecedented fanfare. Gerry had been head football coach and a perennial winner at Moeller in Cincinnati, a Catholic high school that supplied Notre Dame with many of its football stars. He was a surprising choice in 1980 to replace Dan Devine, who had replaced Parseghian. (Devine's Notre Dame experience had led him to comment that "there are two kinds of fans—those that love Notre Dame and those that hate it. And they're both a pain in the ass.") Gerry had never coached a college game; nonetheless by the time he moved to South Bend, he was rumored to be a combination of Knute Rockne, Abe Lincoln, and St. Francis of Assisi. And after his first college game, in which Notre Dame defeated LSU and became ranked number one, there was talk around town of a possible canonization. The Fausts were feted and flattered, until they floundered.

To the dismay of the locals, Gerry was a mere mortal. The team finished the season 6–5. Three years into his five-year contract, "Oust Faust" signs were prevalent and the University was being pressured by alumni to buy out the remaining two years. A poignant photograph of Gerry leaving the field after a loss with his arm around the weeping Marlene appeared on the sports page. Gerry and Marlene looked so innocent, so fragile, so transparent. Neither had developed a sophisticated public persona to present to the critical world. Father Hesburgh refused to surrender to the pressure to fire Gerry, and after two more years, Gerry left Notre Dame symbolically tarred and feathered, the fickle fans poised to embrace his replacement. Gerry was the same ordinary good guy he was when he arrived and said he never regretted his Faustian choice to trade the security and respect he had at Moeller for a chance to coach at Notre Dame.

In South Bend, attention is riveted on Notre Dame sports, especially football. On football weekends the town's population swells by about 50,000 people. A room in South Bend is as rare as an extra ticket to the game; hotels as far away as Michigan City, fifty miles from South Bend, are fully booked. During the football games, the roads and shopping malls are deserted as nearly everyone is either attending the game or watching it on television. South Bend taverns and restaurants sport names like "The Linebacker," "Gipper's Lounge," "Coach's." An alien would think the football coach was president: his picture hangs prominently in so many barbershops, stores, and restaurants. There's no escaping it.

Basketball was certainly a lesser light, but if you coach a

major sport at Notre Dame, in South Bend you're the coach all the time. And if you're the coach's wife, you're that all the time. I tried not to wince when people called me "Mrs. Coach" or "Mrs. Digger"; I was sure I could have been replaced by some other "cute, little blond" at Dick's side and few people would have noticed.

I was fearful of the relationship between success on the court and friendship, and I preferred no friends to superficial ones who might disappear if the team began to lose. There may be many advantages to becoming a head coach at twenty-nine, and a head coach's wife at twenty-six, but social life isn't one of them. We had a great deal of trouble finding people close to our age who treated us normally—as friends, not as Digger and his lovelywife—whose friendship would transcend a losing season.

I survived my anxiety during that first year by the promise of the next. Notre Dame would be at last accepting women as undergraduate students and I applied as a transfer student. Assistant Dean Waddick found my transcript odd—109 credits—three years as a biology major at Rider College and a single year as an English major at Fordham. He found my grades convincing, though, and welcomed me into the College of Arts and Letters.

Thus, in 1972, the year that Notre Dame became a coeducational institution (one of the last to succumb), I entered as a junior. I arranged my schedule around nursery schools and baby-sitters and often selected classes because of when they met rather than what was taught. I was frequently the only woman in my class, and as a blue-jeaned (sometimes mini-skirted, I blush to confess), youthful-looking twenty-seven-year-old, no one suspected I was anyone's wife, let alone the basketball coach's wife. As the sole woman in a class, I would have professors turn to me during class discussions and ask, "Miss Phelps, what is the woman's point of view on this subject?" I was so in awe of the professors that I supposed, initially, that my failure to come up with a different, noticeably feminine, viewpoint signaled a lack in me. I was also too embarrassed to correct the "Miss" to "Mrs."—married women did not attend Notre Dame. Bad enough I was a woman, but a *married* woman student—a mother even—that would make me too much of an oddity.

This atmosphere, in which I thrived intellectually, awakened in me a slumbering feminism, not only because I was supposed to be the bearer of the woman's point of view, but because, I quickly discovered, across the street in the athletic department, I was supposed to be nothing more than the bearer and caretaker of children. People were shocked that I stepped outside my pre-scribed role as a coach's wife; gossip filtered down to us about "poor Digger having to do the grocery shopping" or "Digger has to take the children to his office while Terry's in class."

"So don't do the grocery shopping!" I snapped when Dick related the former remark to me. "I can do it. Big deal!"

"That's not the point. I love to do the grocery shopping. I didn't tell you about that gossip to bother you."

"Don't tell me then. It bothers me. I'm always worrying what people think of me. Sometimes I feel as if I have claustrophobia in this town. I wanted so much to live in a college town—that's what I didn't like about Penn and Fordham—everyone was so spread out. So now I'm in a college town and my life is public property." I burst into tears and began to slam the canned goods that Dick had bought into the pantry.

"Sorry I mentioned it. It doesn't bother me. If I want to do the grocery shopping, I'll do the grocery shopping—Philadelphia, New York, or South Bend. By the way, I got that tuna for ten cents less than our usual kind. Don't overreact."

I spun around to face him. "Overreact? Ten cents? You really don't care what people say, do you? I do all the worrying, for both of us." I was overreacting, of course, to something as trivial as grocery shopping. But my fears went deep. Dick and I were unsuited for scrutiny in a town like South Bend; we were too unconventional and too stubborn to alter our behavior. The somewhat contentious side of me refused to be overshadowed by the amiable coach's wife persona that I thought I would wear with ease. As a Notre Dame student and graduate, I saw the University as partly mine; what it did was partly a reflection of who I was. When the local alumni office sent me announcements for social events that asked me to check the box if I was bringing my wife, I circled "wife" in red ink and wrote that some recent Notre Dame graduates had husbands instead of wives. If they were having a little trouble adjusting to having female graduates, I stood ready to help them out.

Beyond that, most of my close friends were men—a fairly natural phenomenon in the nearly all-male Notre Dame academic environment. I studied with them, ate lunch with them, drank beer with them. People talked and I knew it. Dick, likewise, had close women friends—Mary Ann Roemer, Jane Pitz, others I didn't know. I encouraged him to develop friendships with women; I thought it would be a good antidote to the macho sports world. People talked and I knew it. Sometimes I even heard it.

To say that those early years were hard on our marriage is almost too much of an understatement to make. Dick was rarely home, recruiting constantly in his effort to build the program. I juggled small children, my class schedule, and too little money, often with a growing resentment for the demands his job put on our family. I began to think that the priests not having families made them oddly blind to what they expected of those who worked for them—the cost to family life. Our marriage buckled and nearly snapped under the strain, and were it not for the support of some of our new friends, my memoir of my life as a coach's wife would be much shorter.

In fact, many coaches' marriages do end in divorce, often brought on by the public nature of the job, by the time demands, by the constant pressure, and by the continual public scrutiny. My files from my days of research for *The Lovely Wives* reveal many fears for marriages: of lives filled with loneliness and intense pressure, of loss of privacy and unfair criticism, of the trouble making friends or knowing who real friends are, of family life taking a back seat to the job, of "mushrooming" marriage problems. One wife wrote bitterly of the "groupie" problem—how some women are so attracted to men in sports that they throw themselves at them: "My husband is gone so often and I know those women are out there. Frankly, it scares the hell out of me." The coaches' wives who had survived a decade or more wrote of the necessity for independence and self-sufficiency. Or they wrote of the need for a measure of self-sacrifice that made me cringe to read. I was not alone, then, in what I experienced in those early years. But I thought I was. Coaches' wives did not, still do not as far as I know, get together, air their problems, and gather strength from one another. No, they smiled, and continue to smile, and some, as a few of the returned questionnaires mentioned, turn to alcohol or pills for solace.

Had we lived in a place where marriage is considered disposable, I am certain ours would not have lasted. But, through luck, we found ourselves in a community where people worked on staying married, and we found people who would remain our friends through losing seasons. Mary Ann and Jim, and many other Notre Dame people who entered our lives, helped us to understand that and helped us to work out our differences when the pressures of basketball and fame and all the other new things that were suddenly thrust upon us came close to driving us apart.

Once Mary Ann and I sat on the beach at the lake on campus when I met her son Dan for the first time. "What a great kid he is, Mary Ann," I said as Danny walked away.

"My children are my biggest, my best, achievement," Mary Ann replied with some pride. "I never feel as though I sold out because I'm a wife and mother."

"It's complicated. It's so easy to feel that I should choose between being either an entirely independent woman *or* someone's wife and mother. There sure aren't many role models around here. I mean, I want to get my Ph.D. but I get the feeling that lots of people think I should just concentrate on being the coach's wife. That's all I wanted to be once, but I guess I'm not so good at giving over my identity to someone else. If I get called 'Mrs. Digger' one more time, I'm going to scream."

"Don't throw out the baby with the bath water. You can do both, even if that means you're the first person at Notre Dame to do it."

I watched Mary Ann raise her children and copied her; I observed her assert her own independence against Jim's traditional role expectations, and him painfully adapt to more equality in their marriage. Dick and I learned to invent compromises, as they did. We found that Notre Dame was a place that attracted people like Jim and Mary Ann who cared profoundly for their friends and their relationships.

If I had not come to the Midwest and Notre Dame eagerly, I settled in with a vengeance. I learned to say "pop" instead of "soda"; I learned to ask for a "sack" rather than a "bag" for my groceries. I invited my evening seminar class to meet at our house; a series of undergraduate women lived with us to help me with the children and some of the household chores. Students, players, faculty walked in and out of our house with regularity. We never moved out of that house although having three teenagers and one bathroom put us to the test.

Finally, none of the gossip about my role as a coach's wife affected me; I *loved* going to school. Being allowed to sit and discuss T. S. Eliot, and existential novels, and Milton, and American political philosophy—I could go on and on—I was in heaven. Meeting people who searched out their spirituality, who dedicated their lives to social justice, I began to share Dick's love for Notre Dame—for very different reasons. I remained indifferent to the football team's won–lost record, but I discovered my own truth about the Notre Dame mystique. It existed in the classrooms, in the Campus Ministry office, in the Center for Social Concerns.

Notre Dame was a place, as Norman Mailer once said, where you could talk about the soul without feeling embarrassed.

In that second year, my first as a Notre Dame student, the initial signs of illness appeared. In October I was halfway through my first semester, caring for the children's needs between classes, frantically scheduling classes around nursery schools and day care around classes. I worked constantly, really not knowing if I had what it took to succeed as a Notre Dame student. As I rushed to class, I began to trip, to drop my books. I worried that people would think I was drunk or on drugs. When I studied late after I had fed, bathed, and tucked in the children, the words blurred before my eyes and sometimes disappeared altogether. I'm just exhausted, I thought. I'm trying to do too much. It's nothing. "Nothing" developed into a pronounced numbness through my left arm and leg and I broke down and saw our family doctor. He referred me immediately to a neurosurgeon who, after examining me, wanted to admit me right away for tests. "I can't go in the hospital!" I protested. "We're having weekend guests in for the football game."

Like many people in South Bend, we filled our house with guests for every home football game. We wanted to share the excitement of a Notre Dame football weekend with all of our old friends. I conducted tours of the campus: the beautiful Sacred Heart Church with its Pietà by Ivan Mestrovich, the Grotto where candles lit for prayers flickered day and night, the two lakes with ducks landing in an easy glide across the water, the "Huddle" snack bar, and, of course, the fabled Golden Dome. Then I'd take them to basketball practice, leave those who wanted to stay, and walk the others the mile through our neighborhood adjacent to the campus back to our house, past Moose Krause's house, the Valdiserris', the Derwents', the McFaddens' where Vic had hung an Irish flag to mark the start of a football weekend. I'd serve drinks and disappear into the kitchen to prepare dinner. "Oh, no," I'd say when they wanted to take us out, "all the restaurants are too crowded. Besides we need to eat in time to make it to the pep rally at seven o'clock." I prided myself on sleeping as many as thirteen people and spent the weekdays washing piles of sheets and towels. I'd clean and wash and cook between classes and caring for the children, and I'd love every minute of it. "I have no idea why I'm so tired," I protested to the doctor. He was kind enough not to laugh. He was not pleased about waiting until after the weekend but finally agreed that I could enter the hospital on Monday—after my guests had left.

I tried to put it out of my mind, but underneath I was terrified. I knew he suspected a brain tumor, or at least needed to eliminate the possibility of one. I calmed my fears and submitted to a myelogram and spinal tap. Eight days later, after a dreadful reaction either to the tests or to the medication I was given for the pain caused by the tests, I left the hospital, unable to lift my head for more than a few minutes and having lost fifteen pounds. Although Dean Waddick offered me the opportunity to take incompletes in my courses, I stubbornly refused. The tests revealed nothing specific, and the doctor insisted I slow down, saying that the symptoms would reappear if I pushed myself. I promised to cut down on the number of classes I took and to be more sensible.

But when I registered for classes for the second semester, I saw the light of my degree at the end of the tunnel. If I took six classes, only one more than first semester, and two classes in summer school, I could graduate in August! I enrolled in all six and told everyone, including the doctor, that I had cut back. I ignored the numbness, quit playing tennis, tried to get more rest, and met my scheduled graduation, with high honors. When the numbness reappeared, as it did frequently, I told no one.

But that had been eighteen years ago and somehow we held it all together. Karen and Jenny, now grown up, arrived to help me prepare for the graduation dinner we were hosting for the players and their families that night. "Where's Dad?" Jenny asked as she expertly scraped carrots and sliced celery for a vegetable platter. She and Karen had assisted me with dinners and parties since they were old enough to wield a knife or carry a tray.

"He's doing some shopping for me at the Farmer's Market."

"Say no more. We won't see him for hours." Dick grew up as an undertaker's son in a small town where everyone knew everyone else. He knew the butcher, the baker, the candy store owner on Main Street in Beacon, New York. So he did the same in South Bend. He loved the Farmer's Market and rarely missed going there any Saturday he was in town. First he walked our chocolate labrador around the lakes on campus—more to watch the sun rising over the Golden Dome than for Cadbury's sake. He and Cadbury invariably stopped off at the priests' cemetery where he consulted, so he said, our friends Bill Toohey and Mike McCafferty, both Holy Cross priests who had died.

One October day nearly a decade before, Bill went suddenly into a coma—caused by a rare strain of encephalitis. For ten days Jane, Fitz, and other friends stood vigil at St. Joseph's Hospital, not far from our house. The children and I kept a large pot of soup on and a supply of fresh bread to feed them when they occasionally slipped away from their futile watch by Bill's room.

This lasted—their waiting and our feeding them—until his brain waves stayed flat and the life support was removed. Bill's funeral was the largest since Knute Rockne's, with an unbroken line of mourners stretching from the church to the priests' cemetery half a mile away. Dick and I were pallbearers, and the children stood nearby and watched as we lifted the weight of Bill's casket from the hearse to the graveside.

Mike McCafferty was my good friend on the law school faculty. Young, handsome, debonair: my colleague Tex Dutile joked that Mike was the only priest he knew who sent back the wine at Mass. Mike was among the small group of Holy Cross priests who were possible successors to Father Hesburgh. But

Mike developed lymphoma shortly before his fortieth birthday. I sat in his office just before he left for a last-effort bone marrow transplant. "I know it's going to work, Mike, you have to get better."

"If there's a trump card in the deck, Terry," he said, "I'll find it." It was as if Mike knew how much he meant to all of us; he seemed less attached to life than we were all attached to him. He died with incredible grace and faith in God. He was a teacher to the last, teaching us all how to die.

It was in those times of overwhelming grief that the true Notre Dame emerged for me, the Notre Dame that might be obscured at times by pettiness and ambition. In times of great sadness, I had witnessed the very best that was Notre Dame in a spiritual and emotional coming together that transcended all personalities, all egos. Beneath (or above) the arrogance of "God Made Notre Dame #1" were utter humility and perpetual faith in the face of the ineffable.

Bill and Mike were buried in the priests' cemetery on the fringe of the campus, and Dick would walk with Cadbury along the rows of neat white crosses and pause to talk to them. "So where were you guys?" he sometimes said after a loss. "You're supposed to be paying attention up there and helping us out."

Dick then went to the Farmer's Market where he talked to the butcher, the egg man, the flower lady. Sometimes he distributed extra tickets if there was a game that day. Next he stopped by Macri's Bakery where he chatted with George and Iole Macri, getting all the news of their growing family and sampling the coffee and freshly baked muffins. The Farmer's Market, Macri's Bakery, Parisi's Restaurant, Rocco's Pizzeria—these were his Main Street in South Bend. That's where he found the people with whom he was most comfortable.

That evening I stood at our door to greet the players as my fellow Notre Dame graduates, seventeen years after my own first graduation from Notre Dame. The dogwood blossoms had begun to fall by graduation weekend, and the players, managers, and their families tracked in crumpled blossoms as they arrived for a graduation dinner.

Entertaining players and their parents had become a bewildering process over the years as the web of NCAA regulations governing what we could and could not do for them became increasingly confusing. Although I understood the need for the rules—many schools used any opportunity to gain a recruiting advantage by entertaining players' parents lavishly—the complex regulations made it difficult to be minimally hospitable, to act normal. We dared not become friends with any of the parents because we could not treat them the same way we treat our friends, occasionally picking up a lunch check or inviting them to stay with us overnight at the cottage. But I also knew that it was important to adhere to the letter of the NCAA rules, even when they seemed irrelevant or trivial. We were responsible for setting examples for many young men and bending the rules because we thought they shouldn't apply (even when they shouldn't) didn't provide much of a role model. And, finally, the spirit of the rules was easy enough to comprehend: you couldn't give players anything that the regular students didn't get.

What we tend to forget when we complain about NCAA regulations is that they are an effort to protect *kids*—eighteen- to twenty-two-years-olds. Many of them are from the least advantaged sectors of our society; many, through no fault of their own, are underprepared for college; many come from families with no experience of higher education. If the NCAA doesn't protect them from exploitation, including the short-term, illusory "benefit" of a bribe of several thousand dollars in cash to attend a certain school, who will? So we always tended to be scrupulous about NCAA regulations, checking out the smallest detail, not even doing a gag gift exchange at Christmas with the team unless we knew it did not violate a rule.

Joe Fredrick arrived with several family members in tow. His father is a Notre Dame alumnus and I'd seen his parents frequently at games through the years. Keith Robinson called to say he'd be late because his family was delayed in their drive to town from Buffalo, New York. Keith came in as an NCAA Proposition 48 athlete, one who doesn't make the minimum SAT score and can attend but not play for the first year. He was the first and last because the admissions office said it would not accept any others. I was a bit skeptical myself about his acceptance, but Keith performed well in the classroom at Notre Dame and was graduating with a degree in psychology. Scott Paddock arrived late with his father and brother. Scotty was one of my all-time favorites. He came to Notre Dame as a naive, unworldly kid from Florida and he took a constant ribbing from all of us, particularly my husband, because of his gullibility. He got even, though. One day he entered the track when Dick was doing his very slow jog. Scotty stood watching with a stopwatch for a few laps, then left the track, returned with a calendar, and ostentatiously flipped the pages as Dick trotted by.

Scotty told me how much he'd miss his "Little Brother," a South Bend child with whom Scott has been matched for the last two years. I'm a "Big Sister" and Scott and I have bumped into each other at Big Brothers/Big Sisters functions. Scotty represented some of the best things that athletes can give to a community and set a wonderful example for all the players.

Some players' parents were strangers to me as they lived too far away to visit often or didn't have the money to travel. Many of the parents were poor, and their sons struggled to fit in at a university whose typical student is white and upper middle class. As students at Notre Dame they put up with feeling somewhat out-of-place and uncomfortable in order to get a quality education. Their parents sacrificed seeing a son play at a school closer to home in return for a promise of a Notre Dame education.

With graduation we fulfilled, as best we could, our part of the bargain, and it was clear from the parents' faces that they considered any sacrifice worthwhile. The disappointing season acquired its proper perspective. Basketball was, after all, a game. It was part of what these young men had done here—just a part. The manicured campus was alive with the blossoms of trees and high hopes, perhaps short-lived and easily bruised. Despite the pain of the last month, I knew that what we accomplished here was meaningful, had changed lives. For a moment, for graduation weekend, I could believe in the word *student-athlete*.

PART TWO

SUMMER
1990

"Would you tell me, please, which way I ought to go from here?"

"That depends a good deal on where you want to get to," said the Cat.

—*Alice in Wonderland*

6

You can reach our cottage on Lake Michigan in one of two ways: climb ninety steps or ride a slightly rickety funicular, a blue wooden cable car that slowly labors up the steep hill. That's it. No driveway, no easy way. Climb or ride. When we found the cottage, we were looking for privacy—and found it. No salesmen call at the door, no cars drive by. The lake is on one side, woods on the other three.

We bought this cottage in 1979 as a major compromise. Still partly easterners at heart, we were thinking of buying a house on the ocean but the Jersey shore was too far to travel for short vacations. Lake Michigan was not the ocean, but it had its own mysterious beauty. We wisely gave in to being midwesterners and purchased the cottage, just forty miles from South Bend. The cottage sits precariously on the edge of a great dune; it is literally a house built on sand and the biblical admonition does not escape me. At one time hundreds of yards of sand separated the dune edge from the lake. But the lake, rising each year, has gobbled off huge chunks of the dunes and endangered many cottages, including ours until a few years ago. Now the lake appears to have stabilized and our house on sand is safe. Knute Rockne, the famous Notre Dame football coach, built the original cottage in the 1920s; it has been enlarged by successive owners, but we claim that Knute's ghost still lives here.

When the children were younger and we told ghost stories around the fire, Knute always featured in at least one. "The night he died," we'd whisper, "his family was staying here at the cottage. Just about midnight they heard the funicular climb the hill, slowly, creaking. They weren't expecting anyone so they peered through the fog off the lake. When the funicular reached the top, it was *empty!* What made it come up?"

"Knute's ghost! Knute's ghost!" the children always shrieked. Jenny claimed that he came to speak to her at night and she refused to sleep in the room where, the realtor had told us, Rockne himself had put rope trim around the ceiling. It was also alleged that he invented the forward pass on the beach in front of the cottage. Not true—he *did* invent it, but somewhere in Ohio, I'm told. Still, a great story and, for us, a personal link to Notre Dame's fabled past. We felt part of a continuum, some truth, some legend.

Dick has designated the entry hallway as the "Knute Rockne Memorial Foyer" and has hung collages of old photographs and other Rockne memorabilia on the wood-paneled walls. A South Bend native, who heard we owned Knute's cottage, contributed two scrapbooks filled with newspaper clippings about Rockne to our collection. On the left wall beneath the stairs Dick hung a poster-size replica of the Knute Rockne postage stamp that was issued a few years ago on the hundredth anniversary of Rockne's birth. As a member of the Citizens' Stamp Advisory Board that selects commemorative stamps, Dick pressed for the stamp and organized a spectacular first-day-issue ceremony at Notre Dame. President Ronald Reagan (not as the president but as the "Gipper," Dick insisted) spoke and the Rockne relatives attended. I sat with Rockne's daughter and she sketched out for me the plan of the original cottage.

Summer 1990 was consumed by my writing and Dick's painting. His newly discovered love was painting in oils and he had cleaned out a small attic room to serve as his studio. He combined aspects of Impressionism with the startling colors of the Fauves with the heavy brush strokes of Van Gogh, one of his heroes. He painted and repainted the lake, sunsets, and wonderful, impossible, pink trees. He occasionally called me from my computer to admire his latest creation-in-progress. He was bold about his work, showing it to everyone who came to the house. Our neighbor, Margo Shermeta, is an artist and she confided to me that Dick's work is quite good. "I was afraid," she said, "when he asked me to look at it and tell him what I thought. I thought I would have to make up some half-hearted compliment. But it's not bad, not bad at all. It has a freshness, it's unfiltered, he paints what he sees in his mind. Few people can do that."

I knew. It was hard enough for me to write what was in my mind and I always seemed to select topics that frightened me a little. I am not like Dick; I censor what I have to say before I have even found words for it. But I always pushed ahead, some part of me eager to take on the issues that others shirked.

That summer I wrote about slavery, about women in the church, about racism and sexism, about new methods of teaching minority students, all topics that cut close to my bones. I could not approach them with academic distance and passion entered my writing, passion that exposed me, as Dick's painting exposed him. Exposure worried me—that risk never crossed his mind. Perhaps that was why he was able to work in front of thousands, to be so public, to err and succeed with the world watching. My summer work drained me emotionally, but at least it forced me to focus on my own work instead of fretting about Dick's situation at Notre

Dame—one that was clearly out of my control.

Perhaps influenced by Dick's bold approach to painting, I decided to call a talk that I was preparing for a fall series of lectures at Saint Mary's College, the women's college across the street from Notre Dame, "Looking for Mr. God." I was playing off Judith Rossner's book *Looking for Mr. Goodbar*, a risky analogy that might sound blasphemous to conservative ears. But I wanted to talk about the male image of God that is thrust upon us by most Western religions and how that image can be confusing and alienating for women. I began by explaining that when I was a little girl, living with my paternal grandmother, she taught me to say my prayers. Each night after the customary "Now I Lay Me Down to Sleep" and "Our Father," she taught me to say, "And God bless my father in heaven," a remembrance of her son, my father, who had been killed in the war. Because her house was filled with pictures of my father, many of him dressed in his pilot's uniform, my early image of God, confusing *our* Father with *my* father, was a man in a pilot's uniform, a man I looked like. I was certainly created in that God's image. I outgrew the confusion, of course, but nonetheless my adult spiritual quest for God had too often been dominated by this male image of God the Father. It was only when I could break the bonds of male imagery that I began to feel a connection with God that was not merely that of a child to a parent, or of a subservient woman to an authoritarian man.

I was not much for speaking out on issues such as this, although, as one of the first women students at Notre Dame, I had been involved in some of the early attempts at women's groups. They faltered—or I did. There was not much point fighting that all-male history and tradition; Notre Dame was not yet truly coeducational. It remained a men's school which allowed women to attend. I cooled my ardor, at least publicly, and posted an excerpt from W. H. Auden's "Atlantis" in my library carrel: "You must learn to behave absurdly enough/To pass for one of the boys."

But in 1988, I won a fellowship and spent a year at Yale Law School where instead of being seen as a radical feminist, as I was at Notre Dame, I was seen as moderate, middle-of-the-road. As I worked on a paper about battered women, I discovered that women's silence has contributed greatly to their oppression, that when they have dared to break silence, to tell their stories, change in their lives and in society becomes possible. While at Yale in the midst of this work, I received a letter from John Houck, a colleague on the Notre Dame faculty. He wrote that he had recently met with a student who wanted to talk about her job prospects. During their conversation, she revealed that she really wanted to be a Catholic priest and that the church's refusal to ordain women caused her terrible pain. She bore the pain alone; at Notre Dame the issue was rarely raised. My colleague was writing to a number of us to try to form a committee that would raise the issue of women's ordination, to break the silence.

The official University wanted nothing to do with such a committee. The new administration was reluctant to challenge the Catholic status quo and seemed to prefer that we all forget about women's ordination. I knew that to put myself in a position adversarial to the University was not prudent politically, but I did have tenure and perhaps it was time to demonstrate some moral courage. So I told John that I would join him in his efforts. During the following year, the one just past, the committee had sponsored numerous panel discussions, lectures, and other events. The organizers had asked me to participate on the opening panel and I had found myself the first person that year to speak out publicly at Notre Dame on the issue of women's ordination.

Dick, Karen, and Jenny attended, supporting me from the first row of the library auditorium. Since I expected that a handful of people would attend, the packed room of several hundred surprised and unnerved me. In my brief talk I explained that I did not speak as a theologian or as any kind of expert on church matters; I spoke as a Catholic woman, pained by her church's sexism but willing to fight it out from within. "This is my church, too," I said. "The church that has marched in the streets for equality and justice, that has fed the hungry, and sheltered the homeless—my church, too. Although it would be easy to throw up my hands in despair at the church's intransigence regarding women and to find another church, I am not ready to do that. We are here to call our church to conscience—and we will not go away."

My own words startled me. My place on the stage amazed me. Dick winked at me from the first row and my daughters glowed with pride. Who is this woman who dares to speak like this, I wondered? Not the one who arrived frightened and unsure at Notre Dame nearly two decades ago. Not the one who sat on the beach with Mary Ann wondering how she could ever accomplish all she hoped for. I had somehow managed to ignore all the "I shouldn'ts," all the "I couldn'ts" that came both from outside and, with at least equal force, from within me. In the cradle and crucible of Notre Dame, I traded a mini-skirt for academic robes, endless questions for an occasional answer. And Dick, despite his sporadic discomfort with it all, never uttered a single word of discouragement. In fact, he helped me believe in myself—it was what he was good at. Norman Mailer was right: Notre Dame made *me* the kind of person who could talk about the soul without feeling embarrassed.

Thus began my year of living dangerously, a year that culminated with the University's telling Dick that his services were no longer wanted or valued. It was a relief to escape into summer days of gardening and writing. I was clearing the land, reclaiming a garden from a patch of woods. It was part gardening and part archeological dig as I uncovered old stone steps, paths, and walls beneath years of unraked leaves and undisciplined weeds. I discovered wildflowers that I had never seen before and their appearance made me reluctant to pull up anything without knowing what it was. I turned down the pages of my wildflower book, page after page: dog-toothed violets, bellworts, columbine, and may apples. I mouthed the names over and over and they dropped like treacle from my tongue. These flowers live for an astonishingly short time—some for just a few days—and I had never seen them before because my stays at the cottage had not coincided with their fleeting spring appearances. As my baffled self merged with the earth, the water, the trees and flowers, the trials of South Bend and Notre Dame retreated into the distance.

And better Notre Dame memories replaced them. The cottage was the traditional site for our annual Labor Day lake parties for the team. We invited the basketball team and staff, as well as some of my colleagues from the law school and assorted other friends. Our friends still laughed about the time that Tim Andree, the senior center, rowed the new freshman center, Joe Kleine, far out onto the lake. Joe had arrived at Notre Dame as a hot blue-chip prospect, and already rumors were flying about him starting at center before the season was over. As our little rowboat containing the two big players grew smaller and smaller against the horizon, our friends began to speculate that Tim intended to fake an accident and drown Joe, the only sure way to guarantee his starting assignment for his senior year. "There's no way they're both coming back, Digger," they started in. "Looks like you're back to a single center." Tim, of course, was being friendly to the new kid and was blissfully unaware of the macabre intentions attributed to him by the watchers on the beach.

Perhaps Tim should have worried. At the beginning of Joe's freshman year, his father thought he should be starting rather than going into the game off the beach. He *was* talented and it wasn't too far into the season when he began to start the games. Then Mr. Kleine thought that Joe wasn't getting the ball enough and wasn't scoring enough points. Dick disagreed—Joe was a freshman on a team that included Kelly Tripucka, Orlando Woolridge, Tracy Jackson, and John Paxson—and refused to make the recommended changes. After the season, on Mother's Day in the middle of our family celebration, Dick's assistant Danny Nee called Dick at home to summon him to a meeting that afternoon with Joe and Mr. Kleine. If Joe stayed at Notre Dame, Mr. Kleine said he would never speak to his son again. Dick knew then that Joe would, and should, transfer. He landed at the University of Arkansas.

Fathers. Mr. Branning, Rich's father, gave up a job and moved to South Bend when Rich came to Notre Dame just so he could see Rich play all the time. But he died of cancer before Rich completed his senior year. Mr. and Mrs. Salinas were so proud that their son, Gilberto, was the first Mexican-American to play for Notre Dame, but they were even more proud when they watched him receive his Notre Dame degree. That year we hosted a postgraduation celebration at the cottage for the players and their families; two carloads of Salinases showed up for the party, having driven all the way from San Antonio to see their Gilberto graduate. Then on the return drive, after one of the happiest moments of his life, Mr. Salinas and two other members of the family were killed when their car crashed into a truck stopped along the side of the road, just two hours outside of San Antonio.

Orlando Woolridge's father called every Sunday morning during Orlando's freshman year to discuss why his son hadn't played more. His calls came so regularly that when the phone rang on a Sunday morning after a game, I picked it up and said, "Good morning, Mr. Woolridge." Orlando, at only seventeen, was all arms and legs on the court. He had not been highly recruited, with only Notre Dame, LSU, and Oklahoma offering him scholarships. He, perhaps more than any other player, blossomed at Notre Dame.

Mothers, too. Kelly Tripucka's parents came to many of the games. Frank Tripucka, a star football player for Notre Dame in the forties, sat quietly in the stands and said little about Kelly and basketball. Mrs. Tripucka, on the other hand, had a large cowbell that she rang as she ran along the side of the court if a call went against her son Kelly.

My friendship with Maureen Kempton, Tim's mother, grew out of an embarrassing faux pas. Dick asked me to come along to a recruiting dinner the night that the Kemptons were visiting the Notre Dame campus during Tim's senior year in high school. He asked me tentatively because he knew how I felt about recruiting. For years I was heavily involved and eagerly chatted up prospective players. But I swore off recruiting when Kent Benson went to Indiana instead of Notre Dame. Recruiting can break your heart and recruiting for Notre Dame basketball has hidden obstacles. The typical "blue-chip" recruit is urban, non-Catholic, an indifferent student, quite probably a minority, and with an ego the size of Montana. Dick managed to talk some of them, while they are still in high school, into taking the third year of math that Notre Dame (unlike nearly all other Division I schools) requires for admission. Then he convinced them that they're going to love playing basketball at this primarily white, Catholic school in the wilds of Indiana where football is the major sport.

There are local jokes about the dominance of football. "What would happen if Notre Dame basketball won the national title five years in a row?"

"It still would be a football school."

"What are the two major sports at Notre Dame?"

"Football and interhall football."

It's not even easy to argue that the quality of education is superior. Many of the traditional basketball schools (unlike the football schools), such as Duke, North Carolina, and UCLA, have excellent academic reputations, as well as nearly half a century of basketball as their major sport. I could contribute to recruiting by talking about the superb education available at Notre Dame with some credibility since I attended Notre Dame and taught there. But it was hard for me to stay objective and not to feel personally disappointed when a player I'd become fond of chose another school.

That was what happened with Kent Benson. The children

and I had gotten close to Kent and his family; I still have the
stuffed animals that Kent's sisters made for Karen and Jenny.
Kent even wore a Notre Dame medal that Dick had given him for
good luck throughout his senior season. I liked him and was sure
he would come to Notre Dame. But we came in second. The
Bensons lived in southern Indiana and that is IU country. When
Kent announced he was attending IU, I made my own announcement: "I am finished with recruiting. It hurts too much to be
rejected. Recruiting breaks my heart."

But it was another year and another redhead and I agreed to
go to dinner with Tim Kempton's parents. During dinner one of
the Kemptons mentioned attending a function for police officers
in New York City. I was auditing Tex Dutile's course in criminal
law and was especially interested in police procedures. Consummate feminist, I turned to *Mr.* Kempton and said, "Oh, so you're
a police officer?" I heard a throat clearing on the other side of me.
"Ahem," said Mrs. Kempton, *"I'm* the police officer." I apologized abjectly for my stupid assumption and Maureen graciously
forgave me. I told her about my interest in criminal law. "If you
happen to be in New York sometime and would like to ride along
with me and my partner, let me know," she offered. Maureen was
a uniformed officer in Harlem. I jumped at the chance. "As a
matter of fact, I'll be in New York just after Christmas for a
convention. How about then?"

We made the arrangements; I signed my life away on all the
necessary releases, and the late afternoon of December 27 found
me outside the Essex House on Central Park South asking a taxi
driver to take me to 119th Street, between Park and Lexington,
where I would meet Maureen at her precinct station. The driver
turned around and looked at me incredulously. "Lady, are you
sure that's where you want to go?"

Slightly unnerved at his reaction, I straightened my back,
lifted my chin, took a deep breath, and replied, "I'm sure." I
arrived safely and the next eight hours were among the most

enlightening of my life. I accompanied Maureen and her partner as they responded to over twenty calls, many of them "domestics," in which they were called to stand by while a woman moved out of an abusive situation or they were required to settle a spat that threatened to get violent. They were gentle and nonconfrontational. I was shocked at the conditions in which many people had to live; I was dismayed at the violence children had to witness. Maureen's work was rarely dramatic; in fact, it would have been tedious were it not for the unremitting human misery she saw each day. For me, criminal procedure moved outside the classroom and into the streets. "I love working here," Maureen told me. "I used to work in downtown Manhattan but there everyone just sees the police as hassling them—not letting them double-park their limousines. Up here, the people look to us to help them. They understand that we want to make their lives safer. We're more appreciated."

After midnight Maureen and her partner dropped me off in front of the Essex House. Several members of the Modern Language Association, the convention I was attending, were milling around. As luck would have it so were some basketball coaches since the Holiday Tournament was going on at the same time and the teams were staying at the hotel. I alighted from the police car. As it drove away, Maureen yelled, "And don't let us ever catch you on that street corner again!" Touché. We were even for that first dinner when we met.

Rowing on the lake, pitching horseshoes in the sand, water-skiing if our temperamental boat and the unpredictable lake cooperated. After hours on the beach at the Labor Day parties, the players and our friends climbed back up the dune to the cottage for showers, food, and a Ping-Pong tournament. We drew partners from a hat and one player could end up teamed with the law school dean, with our neighbor's daughter, or even with me. It tended to level the playing field. One senior acted as Ping-Pong commissioner: he made the pairings and moved through the crowd gathered around the barbecue with a clipboard in hand to keep the games going. The grand prizes were always selected from our store of strange Notre Dame memorabilia that people had sent us through the years. My favorite: a "Notre Dame" toilet seat, decorated with shamrocks and equipped with a music box that played the Fight Song when the lid was lifted. Dick and I hated to part with it, but we were running low on prizes.

During the summer Dick left his painting to make recruiting forays when NCAA rules permitted. The NCAA had drastically reduced the number of times that coaches may contact high school players, and a proliferation of all-star camps provided unified sites where nearly all the yearly talent could be viewed at once. When Dick described the Nike camp at Princeton to me, it reminded me of a painful passage in *Uncle Tom's Cabin*, which I was re-reading that summer: "A slave warehouse! Perhaps some of my readers conjure up horrible visions of such a place. They fancy some foul, obscure den, some horrible Tartarus. . . . But no, innocent friend! in these days men have learned the art of sinning expertly and genteelly, so as not to shock the eyes and senses of respectable society. Human property is high in the market; and is therefore well fed, well cleaned, tended and looked after, that it may come to sale sleek and strong, and shining." At these all-star camps, the high school players, many of them African-American, performed under the watchful eyes of coaches, most of them white, sitting in the stands, taking notes on their clipboards: height, weight, points per game, rebounds—all the vital statistics. This camp was not a horrible place, no Tartarus, but there was an auction mentality that permeated the atmosphere. In these days, too, men have learned the art of sinning expertly and gen-teelly. In exchange for so many points per game and wins per season they offer a few years at college, a clean, well-lighted place most unlike the neighborhoods from which many of these players come. They promise fame and fortune in the pros, the imagined destination for every one of the prospects, the real destination for but a few.

Is it wrong that these players get to go to college in exchange for playing ball? Are the camps wonderful opportunities for talented high school players to be matched with suitable schools? Or do they ring uncomfortably of slave auctions? I don't know; they're probably both at once. And if they do have that dual nature, what is our responsibility? That's the key, isn't it? We must take responsibility for what happens to these players. The presence or absence of that responsibility makes all the difference. If more than just a third of these potential players would someday graduate from the colleges now so anxious to recruit them, the question would not be so troubling.

Late in the summer, in the midst of my pondering about slavery, and women, and sports, Dick and I left for the annual Reebok trip, the five-day vacation that the Reebok shoe company sponsors for the basketball coaches who represent it. The shoe company bonus started about ten years earlier when Pony, Nike, Reebok, and other shoe companies decided that they would pay coaches to be their "representatives." In most cases, the coach's team wears the shoes, and the companies thus get lots of television exposure. The money that comes from shoe contracts often exceeds a coach's salary. Only because of shoe contracts were we able to buy the cottage and the same is true for many coaches. One year when Johnny Orr, the Iowa State basketball coach, gave his annual stand-up comedy routine, he said, "I'm sure not goin' to criticize anything Reebok is doing. Romy and I, we got a nice little condominium with 'Reebok' over the door. And we're real grateful for it."

Out of my summer reverie, I was plunged for the next few days among people whose lives are ruled by one of the most male-dominated aspects of culture—sports. It is easy to paint with broad strokes when describing people in sports, but such strokes obscure the truth. The wives, in particular, differ immensely, each finding her own way in this strange masculine world, composing her own life around the rigors and uncertainties of a coach's life.

Some fit the stereotype more than others, basking in their husbands' reflected glory. They seem to enjoy the role of coach's wife, to be content with their lives and their assigned parts. They are gallant, cheerful wives, saying the right things and smiling at the inevitable "Do you get to go to *all* the games?" question. Their own lives revolve around the sport: they help actively with recruiting; they entertain lavishly and are nice to all the right people; they wear the school colors to the games; some even produce their husbands' TV shows. They are truly helpmates in a way that a part of me envied and admired. Part of me wondered if things would have been different for us if I had tried harder to be like that, if I could have been the kind of coach's wife that the fans would have found more acceptable, more typical.

Other wives are more like me: they fight to carve out separate identities under trying conditions. They sometimes have to move abruptly to a new place and abandon their own careers because of a new job for their husband. They bristle, as I have always done, at being called "Mrs. Coach," at being expected to be little more than aging cheerleaders.

Sadly, some wives seem beaten down by it all. Although unable to be expected and typical coaches' wives, they have not found comfortable alternative identities. At these gatherings, their comments are bitter. They sometimes drink too much and laugh too loudly, too shrilly. They hitched their wagons to their husbands' rising stars, and once those stars began to fall, as all do sooner or later, they also seemed to plummet, aimlessly, to earth.

This summer in particular the Reebok group was beset by problems: Paul and Cassie Westhead talked about the tragedy of Hank Gathers's death. The image of Hank collapsing on the court from a heart ailment that everyone thought was under control haunted them. Their grief over his death was genuine, touching, and complicated by the shower of innuendo over Paul's supposed complicity in the decision to let Gathers play. The Gatherses were suing the university for an amount that threatened to dig into the university's endowment. In Cincinnati, a high school player's family was suing because the school *wouldn't* let him play because of a similar medical condition. In California, they sued because Gathers *was* allowed to play. Paul seemed hopelessly caught in the middle—damned if he did, damned if he didn't.

Don Casey told stories of his last few years as he bounced from job to job and the pressures that instability had put on his wife and family. A couple of years ago, when Don was between jobs, Dick invited him to spend the basketball season at Notre Dame so that he could keep his hand in the game while he waited for a new position to develop. Don entertained the group with stories about his winter in South Bend, when he lived in Moreau Seminary on campus in a small, cold, cell-like room, away from his wife and children. "One morning," he said, "I got out of bed and looked out the window for the temperature that day. There wasn't any! No red was showing! No temperature in South Bend that morning!" He could laugh because he was settled into a job with the Boston Celtics, but I remembered when he did not find his situation all that amusing.

Norm Stewart was in the midst of an NCAA investigation at Missouri and spoke bitterly about NCAA tactics. He was buffeted, as well, by pressure to win more. His story struck me as particularly poignant: a former great Missouri player and his wife a former homecoming queen—the darlings of the fans and alumni—until. . . . Until what? Just one day it changes. I wondered what kept these men in coaching, what drive or obsession required that they and their families suffer through such turmoil and uncertainty.

Al McGuire once told me, shortly after he had left coaching at Marquette and gone into television broadcasting, that he most missed the incredible highs and lows, almost like being on drugs. "One day you're on top of the world," he said. "The next day you're playing handball with the curb. It keeps the adrenaline going. I miss that most of all."

Fans seldom see the behind-the-scenes friendship—love even—that exists among coaches. They see only the necessary adversarial posture on the court, the snarling at each other, the requisite sideshow put on for the fans. But a genuine camaraderie existed among all of us, even among those who differed drastically in their philosophical approaches to coaching and recruiting. A camaraderie that sprang from fighting the same war year after year: the reality involved in coaching college kids and the fantasy of fan expectations.

Coaches, finally, have no power and are buffeted about by the hopes of fans and alumni, by the often biased opinions of sportswriters and television commentators, even by the moods of players. Their jobs are on the line game by game. These uncertainties pressure coaches to win any way they can. Alumni and fans are all too willing to turn a blind eye to the means by which a top prospect is induced to enroll at their favorite school; they are also most willing to overlook what happens to that prospect, except for his performance in games; and they rarely show concern for what kinds of athletes play for their school—just so they are top prospects. I often thought that a professional organization, modeled on the American Bar Association or the American Medical Association, might provide coaches with some collective power so that they weren't so tempted to succumb to pressure to win. Such an organization could set internal standards and police itself; it could censure schools that violated coaches' contracts. Then, perhaps, coaches would feel and act like professionals and college athletes would benefit.

Dick, usually more utopian and idealistic than I am, tells me it could never happen. No one wants coaches to have any power—just win games. A major program, such as Notre Dame's, can easily net from $1 million to $2 million for the school; an NCAA bid means an immediate $250,000, just for playing in the first round, with an equal amount added for each win. The teams that make it to the Final Four are richer by at least a million dollars, and a non-conference school, such as Notre Dame, doesn't have to share that money with anyone else. It's direct and unequivocal: if a team wins, the school gets money—a lot of money. Those figures, in times when many schools are struggling to stay out of the red, create a serious conflict of interest. Who pays in the end for those wins? The players who never graduate? The coaches who don't dare play by the rules because they can't win enough games that way? All of us involved in sports who feel we are asked to trade our integrity for a few million dollars? Do we all become a bunch of black dots on the school's balance sheet?

Some of the coaches at the Reebok vacation were clearly on the rise. Having recently won big with a small school, they found themselves in demand, sought after, courted by major programs. I tried not to be cynical as I listened to them. I saw myself, us, not so many years ago and I knew how rough the game could get. I held my tongue, of course. In their seat on the merry-go-round, I would never have believed that the future held anything but gold rings and rainbows.

Our friend John Houck says that fans want sports to be a one-night stand: they want to go to a game and yell and go home, back to their real lives, and forget about it. No real people are involved, no emotions, no commitments, just a few hours of pleasure. Nothing could be further from the truth of what living in a sport is like. *This,* this sport, this *game,* is our real life, and we are very real people. No matter how detached you try to be, no matter how much you try to say "it's just a game," it takes you by the throat, sometimes caressing, sometimes threatening, but always there and always dangerous.

In Dick's second year at Notre Dame, I gave him a gift at the start of the season, a small statue of Sisyphus, the mythic figure whose punishment is that he must eternally push a heavy rock up a hill. Within inches of the top, the rock rolls down, and Sisyphus must push it up the hill again. And again and again.

7

Law school orientation arrived with late August and however unwilling I felt, I had to return to town. Before giving up my summer, though, I went for one last time to Margo's blueberry farm. I had gone there many times during the summer, taking children and friends, to pick and then return to the cottage to make jam and pies from our plunder. Few berries were left on that heavy, hot, late August day; many were beginning to rot on the bushes and the air was filled with the intoxicating smell of decaying fruit. Flies and bees buzzed drunkenly about the bushes, the translucent air purple, like English gin. Although I breathed deeply, I felt no drunkenness, only a deep sadness and I could no longer hold back my tears. Every part of me clung to that place, to those bushes, to the lake, and I dreaded returning to South Bend, to Notre Dame. The summer had given me perspective, distance, and I feared what our return would bring. The future hung like a sword of Damocles. This time next year, I thought, it will all be over. Whatever happens, the waiting will be over. This failed to console me as I filled my pail with the remaining berries, staining my hands and mouth as I picked and ate.

Just days before our summer peace had been abruptly terminated by an unexpected telephone call from Rob Ades, Dick's lawyer/agent in Washington, D.C. A critical scenario had been taking place in South Bend while we relaxed and worked at the lake. We were existing, we knew, inside a fragile bubble of oblivion, breathing only its rarified air, pretending that the events of the spring had not occurred. Rob had called to tell us that he had heard in a conversation with an athletic director at another school that Dick Rosenthal had boasted, more than once, that he was going to "schedule Digger out of a job." Disturbed at what this kind of talk could mean to his ability to negotiate any contracts for Dick, Rob took it on himself to call Notre Dame's lawyer in the hope that the talk could be stopped before it damaged Dick's career further. The power to schedule is surely the power to destroy. Rob had chosen to talk to Notre Dame's lawyer, he told us, because I spoke well of him.

During the past season, LaPhonso Ellis, our premier player, was under terrible pressure because he talked to NCAA investigators about his recruiting by another school. The press made it sound as though LaPhonso had done something wrong; besides, it was his state school that was being investigated and in LaPhonso's neighborhood, in East St. Louis, Illinois, being a "snitch" was not looked upon kindly. LaPhonso felt as though the world was coming down on him and it clearly affected his play all season. Just at the end of the season, he told me that his mother had lost her job. She worked for an alumnus of the school under investigation and he fired her in retaliation for LaPhonso's honesty. This, for me, was going too far. Accustomed as I was to malfeasance on the part of overzealous fans and alumni, this striking back at a player's family crossed a line. But what could I do? I was leery of violating NCAA rules by doing or saying anything to help LaPhonso or his mother. But I was worried about him; he was paying a big price for having been honest. So I asked the university lawyer, who sometimes joined the law school faculty for lunch and who was (I had thought) a friend, if there was anything that could be done. He had been sympathetic and seemingly sensitive to the unpleasantness possible on sports' underbelly. He told me that he would look into it and I trusted him, although he never told me what the outcome had been. I had related all this to Rob in a casual conversation. Thus when Rob puzzled over what to do about what he had heard, he depended on my judgment.

Apparently a big mistake. "Digger's done," Rob was told perfunctorily. "The priests want him out and it's their school and they can do whatever they want." What the athletic director was saying, or was accused of saying, was of no concern to anyone.

Rob is a tough union negotiator with no special feeling for Notre Dame. He was appalled when he discovered some years ago that Dick worked without a contract. "Are you crazy?" he exploded. "You're a college *coach*, for God's sake. They could fire you on a whim!"

"Notre Dame is different," we replied.

At the lawyer's indifference to Rob's concerns, Rob remembered our words. "Notre Dame's not different," he said to the lawyer. "It's just like Oklahoma or any other school."

"Maybe it is," was the reply. "The Ted and Ned years are over."

"So Notre Dame is different?" he asked when he called us at the cottage to tell us the story. Oddly the athletic director's alleged remark gave the scheduling decisions of the last two years some coherence. I had been trying to make sense of it, to create a pattern. Two things became immediately clear: the athletic director would be protected at any cost, and we didn't know who our friends were.

Dick was more shocked than I'd ever seen him, the fight gone out of him. "How can we deal with this kind of thing?" he asked me. "Why don't I just quit and get it over with?"

"Don't!" My response was unequivocal. "You've done a wonderful job at Notre Dame. Your only mistake was treating coaching like a profession, not like a job. You erred by being loyal to Notre Dame, for not leaving ten years ago to make more money, to fry fresher fish. Or cut your losses and run when the going got tough. Or played the threatening-to-go-elsewhere game like Bobby did so successfully when he had a conflict with Indiana's president. No, your very love for Notre Dame has become your fatal flaw. Don't let them make you feel like a failure. You're not."

I whistled Cadbury in from his exploration of the far reaches of the deserted blueberry farm and unwillingly made my way back to the cottage, to wash my purple-stained face and burr-filled hair, to take off my summer and put on a dress, pantyhose, my watch, all the accoutrements of social convention. I packed up the blueberries to be frozen and used for our blueberry pancake breakfasts during the fall.

We had started the blueberry pancake breakfasts in our second year at Notre Dame when, in a burst of idealistic fervor, I decided that the team didn't get enough social opportunities to interact among themselves or with other people on campus. After a few false starts, we got the routine down perfectly. On several Sundays during the fall, Dick arose early to set the table and start his home-fried potatoes. He boiled the potatoes with the skins on and left them in a colander to cool. By the time I was up and dressed, Dick's secretary, Dottie Van Paris, and some of the assistant coaches' wives and the trainer's wife, Pam Meyer, had arrived to take up their positions in the kitchen. One peeled the potatoes and sliced them into a huge frying pan with a chunk of butter. Dick added the precise amount of paprika and salt and relinquished the spatula. He wouldn't tell any of us exactly how much paprika he added; it's the "secret" part of his secret recipe. Pam scrambled the eggs a dozen at a time in the blender, adding her own secret amount of milk and seasoning. Her husband, Skip, arrived a little later with their children, Lindsay and Christopher, whose job was to play with Cadbury in the backyard while we were preparing breakfast. Someone else cooked the bacon, sausage, or ham. Our children did more menial chores: pouring juice, putting milk, butter, and syrup on the table. Rick lighted the wood in the fireplace and put music that (he said) the players would like on the stereo. Jenny, the youngest, made the toast, a fairly error-proof job. When Jenny was sixteen and still making the toast at the blueberry pancake breakfasts, she suddenly complained loudly: "Year after year and all I do is toast. Toast, toast, toast. I want a promotion!" I always presided over the blueberry pancakes and they were the one thing that former players always remembered about me. I was famous for them. Although one year, when Jim Dolan, who played in the early eighties, returned to Notre Dame as a graduate assistant, I got my comeuppance. Jim came into the kitchen one Sunday morning and asked me if I would mind making a few pancakes without blueberries. "Without blueberries!" I said. "You mean you don't like blueberry pancakes?"

He was clearly embarrassed. "Actually I don't. But I was always too afraid to tell you."

The other wives and I relaxed as we took up our routine chores, caught up on each other's lives, and congratulated ourselves that so few of us could serve so much food to so many people, many of them *big* people with large appetites. By the time the assistant coaches arrived with the players, the dining room table was laden. Other guests also appeared: Emil Hofman, the dean of freshman year; the dean of students; a few professors; Holly Martin, a former graduate student friend in charge of academic support for athletes; Father Riehle, the unofficial team chaplain. Former players visiting for a football weekend stopped by the kitchen and indulged themselves in nostalgia for the good old blueberry pancake days. Other guests peeked in the kitchen to ask how *many* pancakes we had served. I tried to be modest: "Several hundred," I'd say.

When John Shumate became an assistant coach and his wife, Marilyn, arrived on a Sunday morning to take up her post in the kitchen, she looked at me preparing the blueberry pancakes and said, "Now I get it!"

"Get what, Marilyn?" I asked while expertly flipping a perfect blue-studded pancake.

"The blueberry pancakes! When I first met John, when he was playing for the Phoenix Suns, he asked me if I knew how to make *blueberry pancakes!* I thought he was crazy!"

And I even pick the blueberries myself, I thought as I tipped the pail of blueberries into freezer bags. It's the secret part of my secret recipe. I shivered. Despite the summer sun coming through my kitchen window, I began to feel as frozen as my freshly picked blueberries would be. I didn't know to what we were returning. More blueberry pancake breakfasts to be sure, but what else? Above all, I didn't know if my advice to Dick was good advice. What if I was wrong? Even worse, what if I was imposing on him my own foolish stubbornness in the face of adversity? Perhaps Notre Dame *was* different—different from what we thought it was. I feared what would happen next.

PART THREE

FALL

1990

"Tut, tut, child," said the Duchess. "Everything's got a moral, if only you can find it."

—*Alice in Wonderland*

8

hat *was* I expecting? As I try to pull together the threads of my memory into a fabric I can see and understand, it occurs to me that there is something about human nature that expects the best, even in the face of contrary evidence. Why else do people futilely resist a fatal disease? Why else do people fight against a clearly dominant enemy? Perhaps I had inherited a blitz mentality from being born in wartime England, a mind-set that refuses to believe that we won't win in the end, despite the overwhelming odds. But, in this case, what was winning anyway? Getting back what we had before? Getting back the old Notre Dame?

And what of Dick? What hope or dread lurked in *his* heart? He rarely spoke of it; we had called a moratorium on discussing "the topic." It was too painful and we both had work that demanded our undivided attention.

Dick always had the ability to concentrate fully on the task at hand, that's why he was so good at preparing for big games. Readying a team for an incoming number-one opponent drew from him remarkable powers of concentration. It is, as he sometimes says immodestly, what he's good at. Our friend (and my former professor) Ernest Sandeen heard this with his poet's ear and wrote a poem about Dick called "The Game and The Word": "Listen, it's day after day,/week by week, I have to be there,/I have to muscle my words/onto their bodies/sweat with the prayers/I lead them in. It's what I'm good at."

Would he be good enough for this? Just getting the team ready for the coming season and completing the work of recruiting a class of players that he was told he could never coach seemed to be his chief opponent. Despite everything, this year's team held much promise. He hoped, I think, that life would return to normal and that he would be given a chance to coach this team to its full potential. Nothing we experienced before prepared us for the year that was to come. We would have to improvise our parts, speaking and acting with no predetermined script.

What really happened, though, was that we became victims of the fatal law of gravity: when you are down everything falls on you. Whatever human agents from which we expected the worst were no match for what happened as soon as we returned to South Bend: Monty Williams's illness.

Consider this. You are a seventeen-year-old who plays basketball well enough to be recruited to play in a major program. The world's your oyster; your future is assured. You will certainly be an All-American and an NBA prospect. You played well as a freshman and earned a starting position. After a summer of lifting weights and working out, you have gone from 205 to 220 pounds—all muscle—you are ready, I mean *ready*, to play.

Then, during a routine physical examination before school begins in the fall, you discover that you have a heart condition that ends your career—hypertrophic cardiomyopathy, a rare condition that involves a thickened muscle between the chambers of the heart—too much heart, you could say. Although you won't be an invalid—you can jog, ride a bike, even shoot a basketball once in a while—the condition carries an unacceptably high risk of sudden death during strenuous exertion—like, say, playing a basketball game.

My own heart ached when I thought about Monty. Of course, his inability to play hurt the team. He was a versatile 6'7" guard, who could play four, maybe five, positions, an excellent ball-handler, passer, and dribbler, who could both score and get the ball to other players. He would definitely have started and would have helped bring out the best in the other players. Losing Monty meant losing at least a couple of close games in which his presence would have made the difference. But teams go on, recover. How does an eighteen-year-old adjust to such a loss?

Mary Ferlic, who teaches social work at Saint Mary's College, uses a class exercise to help her students, future social workers, understand the impact of loss. She gives each student fifteen slips of paper, three each of five different colors. On one color they write the names of three people dearest to them, on another three precious possessions, then three activities they enjoy, three dreams that keep them going, and three important qualities they have. With the students sitting in a circle, Mary asks each of them to hand her one of each color: to give her one of the people, one of the qualities, and so forth. Then, as they fan the paper slips in their hands, she takes one from each of them, forcing them to relinquish control over what they surrender.

After this silent exercise, the students giving colored slips to the omnipotent teacher, they discuss how they feel as they lose each thing. When Mary told me about this class exercise, I felt a pang of loss imagining myself letting go of a slip of paper containing the name of one of my children; or even letting go of a slip containing my ability to teach, to write, to articulate ideas so that others can understand them. Monty was not involved in a classroom exercise; he had not merely turned over a slip of paper containing his ability to play basketball. He was living it. He alone had to learn to live without his dream.

Dick tried to make it easier for him in any way he could. He had Monty talk on the telephone to others in the same situation, sometimes to someone younger so that Monty was forced into the role of consoler and explainer of loss and adjustment. Monty said all the right things to the press, but I knew his heart was not only damaged but broken. When I talked to him, I searched for the right words—as if there were any, as if my words could transcend the powerful social message that makes young men like Monty too sure that their worthiness is encompassed in their ability to play basketball. We talked of all the other things he did well, of how much his Notre Dame degree would mean, of how lucky he was to be at such a good school. Yet even as we talked, he sometimes looked away, his eyes glassy and wet, and my words sounded empty to me. You see, I knew what it was to get such news, what it was to have to give up who you used to be.

Three years ago, just about this time of year, the numbness and vision problems that had plagued me since my second year at Notre Dame reached unignorable proportions. I knew something was *wrong*, no question about it. Since my eyes were the most affected, I started with the eye doctor. He found nothing in particular and prescribed drops for possible dryness caused from reading too many student writing assignments. Usually passive in a doctor's office, this time I rebelled. "It's not dryness," I insisted. "I know there's something wrong." Because I remained adamant, he ordered a test that would go behind my eyes and measure how well my optic nerve was functioning. Even as I watched the machine graph out the response time between my eye and my brain, I could see the manifest difference between my right eye and my left one.

The next morning the doctor called and asked to see both Dick and me at his office as soon as possible. It was now December, shortly before Christmas, in the heat of the beginning of basketball season. I thought briefly of not mentioning the call to Dick, of going alone to the doctor to hear whatever bad news he had to tell us. Schooled all these years as a coach's wife, I worried first about the team, about Dick's concentration as he prepared for the upcoming game. My resolve failed and the two of us sat in a darkened office listening to the doctor say, "I think Terry has multiple sclerosis. I can't be sure but the test showed a kind of damage to the optic nerve that is nearly always caused by myelin deterioration, that is, by MS. We need to take more tests, but I'd be surprised if this were not the case."

He was right. Subsequent tests only exhausted my diminished energy. An MRI, not available as a test when I had first shown these symptoms years before, now revealed the damaged nerves. By Christmas Eve the diagnosis was confirmed. I made it through Christmas and then lay in bed for nearly a week, overwhelmed with fatigue and grief, crying intermittently. The hardest part was the necessary re-visioning of myself. I prided myself on my inexhaustible store of energy; I could work harder and longer than anybody. The self I had imagined was no longer possible. I had to *conserve* energy, not spend it wantonly. I had to *rest*, to choose activities, rejecting some because they would take too much of my strength. I began to realize how much the word *run* was part of my vocabulary: I would "run" to the grocery store; "run" over and visit a friend; "run" home at lunch to do the laundry. I wasn't going to be running anywhere very much, if at all. I learned, as Monty would, that illness is a place where you go alone, no one can keep you company, no one can make it all right, no one completely understands.

Monty was not the first player under Dick's charge to suffer a career-ending or life-threatening injury. In our first year at Notre Dame, the best player on the team was John Shumate. Shu was a great one for dramatics, lingering on the floor whenever he went down during a game, laboriously pulling himself up, his wonderfully expressive face grimacing for the sake of the TV audience. For years afterwards, we kidded about the "John Shumate Award for Dramatics during a Game." It was hard to take him seriously when he complained of pains shooting around his body. Luckily we paid attention, and a subsequent hospital test showed a blood clot in his leg and a viral infection around his heart that made the clot untreatable. He was in critical condition for four days as the doctors feared the clot would move to a more vital area. He was finished for the year and the team was too—that was the 6 and 20 season.

He came back, though. His story is one we like to hear, about the player who overcomes injury and triumphs, the happy myth of sports and life. The next year, his junior year, Shu was MVP in the postseason National Invitational Tournament, and in his senior year he finished second to Bill Walton in the Player of the Year ballots.

But his story didn't end there. The clot came back to haunt him early in his pro career. I think it's fair to say that it took Shu some time to adjust to the loss of his old version of himself—professional basketball superstar. He struggled to imagine a revised self, and in so doing took Dick, at least in part, as his model. He came back to Notre Dame as an assistant basketball coach and then became head coach at SMU.

For Monty there seemed to be no chance to live out the happy myth of recovering and going on to play, although he secretly hoped that another test to be taken in January would show a misdiagnosis. Instead he would probably be more like Ray Martin, who went down during an Indiana game, his ankle bone protruding through his skin. Eleven thousand of us in the ACC watched with horror as Ray was carried on a stretcher from the floor, our concern over the game's outcome foolishly inappropriate in light of what had happened. His playing career was over and he had to find a life outside of playing basketball. That's another version of the myth—the injured player who can't play again but makes the most of his life. Ray did: he's an assistant basketball coach at Tennessee on his way up. He's still in basketball as it turns out, but not in the way he intended as a hot shot kid on the playgrounds of Queens, New York. He revised the script and learned to live it. I didn't know him well enough to detect his internal struggles, but I am sure there were many.

And then there was Mike Mitchell, whose knees got so bad that he hobbled through his senior year, that's how much he wanted to play basketball. In fact, his will was so strong that he took charge of the team one night and upset a highly ranked team from San Francisco, Mike's hometown. Dick gave him the game ball as a testament to the force of will over ability. Mike probably wouldn't have played at all but we were short on talent—that was the 10–14 season, the only losing season Dick had since that dismal first year. But hobbled knees are not professional basketball material and Mike had to find a job outside of basketball. He was becoming a successful businessman and wrote to Dick regularly, generous in his praise for the lessons he learned from Notre Dame basketball: "My foundation in business is built upon integrity, a positive attitude, hard work, attention to detail, organizational skills, realistic goals, confidence, and a burning desire to tackle any situation that arises head on. These characteristics and skills are what you preached and we practiced every day. My knee injury was a blessing in disguise."

But when injuries come, they do not look like blessings of any sort. A few years ago, again just at the start of the school year, we received a 3 A.M. telephone call, that ominous late-night ringing that only portends bad news. I groped for the telephone and heard the team trainer's voice ask for Dick. "My God, Skip, what's wrong?" I blurted out.

"David and Kenny have been in an accident."

Dick snatched the phone from me and learned that two of our basketball players, David Rivers and Ken Barlow, had been hit by an oncoming car at an intersection out in the country. Kenny, who was driving, was not injured, but David had been thrown from the van and a piece of glass had sliced him from one side to the other across his middle. Dick went immediately to the hospital fifteen miles away where David had been taken. He waited through the night and early morning while surgeons assessed the damage and repaired what they could. While he waited, Dick called David's parents in Jersey City, New Jersey, and they prepared for the long drive to Indiana.

David was second youngest of thirteen children and his parents had already seen more than their measure of tragedy. One son had been shot in the streets, another was killed in an automobile accident. Still another, the youngest, would die of a brain tumor in two more years. Dick loved telling stories of recruiting David, of how the family wove a protective web around their star, measuring the worth of recruiters with a probity that would have pleased the FBI. His older sisters were particularly vigilant, the gatekeepers. Dick passed muster with his promise of an education, with his insistence that David was more than just another great basketball player. Having to call them and tell them of David's accident and injuries, Dick said, was one of the hardest moments of his life. David's father would lose pay for missing days at work, but the Riverses had no money for plane tickets. They had no choice but to drive the 900 miles to South Bend. We would have written them a check to cover their fares in an instant if the NCAA would not have come swooping down on us, upholding a rule that still makes no sense to me.

David was lucky. The glass missed his vital organs by a fraction of an inch, but he required a long, hard spell of rehabilitation. During his rehab he developed a relationship with one of our friends, John Houck. John is a brilliant man, a creative teacher, and a character in the truest sense of the word. Early in the summer when David was hurt, John had suffered a near-fatal aneurysm, collapsing in a men's room in the business school. By chance someone found him immediately and administered CPR that surely saved his life. But he was not home free until months later, and when the semester began he still could not return fully to his teaching duties. He could barely speak above a whisper because of the damage that emergency tubing had caused, and he still was afflicted with frequent double vision. He accepted David, who had much academic catching up to do, into a tutorial, and the two of them, both recovering from brushes with death, read law books dealing with social reform together—the boy/man from Jersey City and the professor with his Harvard degree.

Because John had such difficulty speaking, David did all the talking. So David read *Gideon's Trumpet* and *Inherit the Wind* and talked, and talked, and talked. He sat, nearly doubled over from his injuries, across from John in his office, two Davids sometimes swimming before John's eyes, and it all came rushing out. "It was like opening a dam," John told me. "David's high school teachers had done a wonderful job of instilling confidence in that slight boy from Jersey City. But he had been silenced a bit at Notre Dame, where everyone asks about your SAT scores." John, by his own admission, learned as much as David. "That young man has a doctorate in how to grow up in a tough neighborhood," John said.

David played again that year, graduated, and went on to get a pro contract. To me, though, he seemed less aggressive, understandably protecting himself from elbows to his body. He was a great player, but I somehow think that the accident brought him down a notch. That, in addition to his small size, made him a marginal pro player. Dick urged him to go with Larry Fleischer, an agent who represented not only some of our best players, but also our marginal players—guys like Tim Kempton—and did a fine job for them. But David insisted on his independence from his coach and chose a different agent. He bounced from team to team, unable to give up his vision of himself as a pro superstar. Although he technically overcame his injury, he is still struggling to adjust to a different self, one whose pro career might not go on forever.

Through the years I've come to recognize that adjusting to

injury is far more complex than the myth allows us to realize. It is more than, or different from, "overcoming" it. It involves a shedding of the old self, as if of a shell or skin. But, and here's the rub, the discarded self is not one outgrown but one beloved. You do not, for a while at least, move on to being something *more* but something *less*. The adjustment entails finding the ability to re-imagine oneself with the limitations of the injury, to let go of the old self and embrace the new.

And how did I re-imagine myself? I wish that I could say that I *had* done it, had been so successful that I could hold myself up as a splendid example of overcoming—or of re-imagining. But that's not entirely true. Sometimes, yes, I remember to get plenty of rest, to avoid strenuous physical exertion that will lead to fatigue, to say no to one more project. But then time passes and I forget. I do too much expecting Terry, Wonder Woman, to respond. And when I cannot walk well or the fatigue becomes so severe that I feel as though someone has pulled out the plug that attaches me to any energy at all, I collapse into bed for a couple of days, wailing at the unfairness of fate. My imagination has failed, my new self obscured by my nostalgia for the old.

With athletes at Notre Dame, we've mostly known success stories, successful, I think, because David, Ray, Mike, and Shu played in a program that cared about them and their futures, that didn't see them as insignificant once their usefulness on the court was over, for a coach who saw more in them than just basketball players. Dick insisted, too, that the players not see *themselves* merely as basketball players. He would not allow the seniors to begin practice on October 15 unless they had lined up three job interviews. He required these interviews even of those players who were sure (or thought they were) early-round draft picks. He began each practice day with a discussion of current events, forcing the players to remain aware of the world outside the basketball arena. He followed NCAA rules to the letter. "Digger's unrealistic," one of Dick's former assistants said to me once. "You have to give players some extra stuff the NCAA doesn't allow. A charge account at a clothing store, a little spending money now and then. It's expected, it's part of the game."

But Dick meant it when he said he saw his job as preparing them for life—that was what he promised their parents. You cut a class, you're benched for a game, no excuses accepted. One year he heard from Fred Beckman, a friend who was a professor in the art department, that Kenny Barlow had cut Fred's class. Dick went to Kenny's dorm where he lived with teammate Scotty Hicks. Dick knocked on the door. "Yeah, who's there?" Scotty said.

"Open up!" Dick responded.

"Kenny, it's Coach!" Scotty opened the door.

"So, Kenny, I heard you missed an art class."

"Sorry, Coach, I fell asleep."

"You can sleep through the game against Oregon tomorrow night. You're benched." Kenny dressed for the game and watched it from the end of the bench. At the postgame press conference, a reporter asked why Barlow hadn't played.

"He cut a class. You don't go to class, you don't play. That's the rule. He knew it."

You go to classes and you don't drink in public: "Even if you only have one beer," Dick told his players, "and you have a bad game, people will say you're playing bad because you drink. If you want to have a beer, drink it in private. Don't drink in the student bars." He was hard on his players, expected a lot of them, and scared the hell out of them if they messed up—as I discovered one early September morning in the emergency room.

I received a telephone call at 5 A.M. from one of Dick's assistants. "Terry, I've got to talk to Digger."

"Sorry, he's somewhere on the East Coast, sweet-talking seniors just like you are out there in California." September is the height of the recruiting year when coaches try to convince seniors to visit their campuses. Every coach in the country is out talking to high school prospects. "Why are you calling at this hour?"

"I just got a call from one of the players. Gary Voce passed out outside the Commons and they've taken him to the emergency room at St. Joseph's."

"Let me try and find the trainer or one of the other assistants. Don't worry. I'll find someone to get down there."

First I tried Skip Meyer, the trainer. The Meyers' telephone rang and rang until I remembered that they were in Connecticut for a family wedding. So I tried Matt Kilcullen, the other assistant. "I'm not home right now, but if you'll leave your number. . . ."

"Pick up the phone, Matty. Pick it up!" I begged into the receiver to no avail. I ran out of ideas so I pulled on a sweat suit and headed for the emergency room myself.

"I'm looking for Gary Voce," I said. "I'm Digger Phelps' wife. He's one of our basketball players."

A doctor walked up to me looking somber. "Mrs. Phelps, Gary's back here. He's all right. We're running tests but I think he just had a little too much to drink and then started to hyperventilate because he was afraid of being seen drunk."

"You did a drug test?"

"Right away. No problem there. We gave him a mild sedative to calm him down. I just can't get him to relax."

Gary's big frame looked somehow childlike against the white sheets. He was awake and still shaking. He was not particularly thrilled to see *me* walk in but I knew I was much preferable to my husband. *Anyone* was preferable to my husband. I took his hand. "Gary, what happened?"

"I just had a couple of Long Island iced teas at the Commons and I started to get dizzy and then I got scared and then I passed out."

"Long Island iced teas! Do you know what's in those?"

"No. I don't drink much." He closed his eyes and I saw tears form under his lids. The doctor stuck his head into the cubicle. "The test results are back. Nothing's wrong. He's got a friend in the waiting room who can drive him home so we'll release him in a little while."

I was relieved and wanted to giggle at this big kid who just met his first Long Island iced tea. My rite of passage was Manhattans, I thought. Must be something about those New York drinks. I leaned over Gary and put both my hands on his shoulders. "Listen, Gary. As far as I'm concerned this is just between us. Coach doesn't need to hear about it, okay?"

Gary opened his eyes and a huge tear rolled down his cheek. "Thanks."

As we nurtured Monty through his disappointment as best we could, I realized how much that aspect of coaching meant to me. Surely, somehow, this was more important than winning games. Dick was proudest of pages 246–247 in the press guide—titled "The Graduates"—the pages that list where his players were and what they were doing. For me they're the only statistics that matter.

Meanwhile the annual football frenzy had befallen Notre Dame. A football weekend at Notre Dame is truly a sight to behold— college football according to Walt Disney. Small pep rallies in scattered sites around the campus begin on Thursday night. By Friday noon I fight traffic to get to my office in the law school. The "Notre-doters" have arrived—in blue, green, and gold plaid trousers, some even adorned with leprechauns and shamrocks. They flock around band practice and the bookstore, which supplies them with the requisite "God Made Notre Dame #1" buttons and bumper stickers. On Friday night the big official pep rally begins as a crowd of thousands gathers inside Stepan Center—a campus building seemingly constructed for just that purpose—to scream encouragement to the team. The band plays the Fight Song over and over, whipping the already impassioned mob into delirium. The coaches speak, as do several of the football players, although few of their words are heard above the crowd and band. No one cares *what* they are saying, only that their famous faces and magnificent bodies are visible, so that they may be hailed as gods and heroes.

Game day itself starts early Saturday morning with a band performance on the steps of the administration building. The South Bend weather even cooperates as the autumn is our only good season. The trees along Notre Dame Avenue, the corridor that links the town to the campus, glow like Olympic torches in the noon sun. Throngs follow the band as it marches to the football stadium. Students raise money by selling food on the quads, and the parking lots are filled with tail-gaters imbibing bloody marys, fried chicken, and oceans of beer. Inside the stadium, the mosaic library mural, known as "Touchdown Jesus," looms over the wall enclosing the north end zone and small planes fly overhead carrying signs saying "Happy Fiftieth Birthday, Marge" or "I love you, Joan." The game itself seems incidental to the days of partying with old friends that precede it, although a loss can palpably dampen spirits and cast a pall over postgame get-togethers. Notre Dame is supposed to win—it's that simple.

In 1990, however, a cloud floated over Notre Dame football. *Sports Illustrated* had run a story about a former player who alleged steroid misuse among Notre Dame football players. Notre Dame officials scrambled like Keystone Kops to undo the damage. The athletic director fumbled through a press conference in which he denied the story. Father Beauchamp appeared on the late news to say he fully supported Lou Holtz and that he could stay at Notre Dame as long as he chose.

The basketball schedule for the coming year was finally made public. It contained fifteen road games (one fewer than last year) and only twelve games at home, including two home stands when the team would play four games in eight days. Most coaches try to play a few more games at home than on the road. And so did we until last year. Dick was concerned about his players' ability to perform in the classroom under those conditions. The "student" part of "student-athlete" appeared lost in the rush. But he could do nothing; the schedule was no longer his to design. It seemed as though Dick's choice had become to re-imagine himself as a coach less concerned with education—or to re-imagine himself as something other than Notre Dame's basketball coach.

PART FOUR

THE SEASON

1990–91

"Now, *here,* you see, it takes all the running *you* can do, to keep in the same place. If you want to get somewhere else, you must run at least twice as fast as that!"

—*Through the Looking Glass*

9

And so it began once more. Golden October declined into somber November and the sky dropped like a clouded bell jar. As inevitably as the first South Bend snowfall, and less welcome as far as I was concerned, the basketball season commenced. Practice began, as usual, on October 15, the date designated by the NCAA. Some coaches make a big event of the October 15 date and have a "Midnight Madness" practice at one minute after midnight on the 15th to psyche up the students for the coming basketball season. Anything to create frenzy in the fans.

The playing season usually began about six weeks later around December 1. Our season that year started earlier than usual as we were playing in the preseason National Invitational Tournament (NIT), which included a field of sixteen teams. The first two games were played at local sites and the four survivors of these first two rounds traveled to New York City for the semifinals and finals over the Thanksgiving holiday. At one time the NIT was a powerful postseason tournament, a close second to the

NCAA, and sometimes the winner of the NIT was considered the best team in the country. That was until television coverage transformed the NCAA tournament into a superevent and the postseason NIT became a tournament for also-rans. The NIT managed to get the best teams by initiating another tournament before the season, during which the television audience got a preview of the season to come.

I had an ambivalent, maybe hypocritical, reaction to our playing in the NIT. On the one hand, in my coach's wife persona, I was happily anticipating a trip to New York if we could win the first two games. On the other hand, as a member of the faculty, the very existence of this preseason tournament infuriated me. It forced the long basketball season to start even earlier, allowing the players still less time to be anything remotely resembling students. In many ways, this tournament graphically demonstrates how money has come to drive college sports. Our players competed until late March as it was, and now, because we could make more money, we made them start two weeks before the standard December 1 tipoff date. So much for academics or any real hope that they could get an education as well as a degree.

I was proud of Dick's record of graduating players at Notre Dame. His 100 percent loomed over the rates at other schools: 33 percent nationally, an even more shocking 26 percent for minorities. Getting a degree *is* important. But getting a degree is not necessarily the same as getting an education. Just two weeks ago Rosa Parks, the heroine of the Montgomery bus boycott, came to speak at Notre Dame and Dick encouraged his players to attend to hear her. I copied pages from Taylor Branch's *Parting the Waters* that describe Parks's central role in defeating the Jim Crow laws in the South and Dick distributed copies to the team. Dick let the team out of practice early so that they could make the seven o'clock lecture. Unfortunately, a crowd had been gathering since six o'clock and the room for Parks's talk was too small to accommodate the overflow. Because practice, even a foreshortened practice, prevented them from arriving earlier, there was no room for our players to hear Rosa Parks speak.

We sell athletes and their families a bill of goods and because many athletes come from families with little experience with higher education, we get away with it. We make them feel privileged to be allowed to attend our schools and make millions of dollars for us—as well as nourish the egos of our win-hungry alumni. In return, we let them go to class as long as the classes don't interfere with their practicing or playing. They usually cannot take challenging classes because those classes might hinder their eligibility to play. They cannot participate in most extracurricular activities available to regular students because the team comes first. Even off-season requires demanding hours working out and lifting weights. Imagine yourself as a student at a university with rigorous academic standards, having to put in three or four hours daily for a sport. In addition, you will miss entire days of class to travel to away games. Not easy to imagine doing well, is it? Yet we persist in calling them "student-athletes." Why? Because it makes us feel better.

The solutions are obvious, but they run counter to the driving force in college sports in the nineties—making money. First, eliminate freshman eligibility. Give these students, many of whom are ill-prepared for college thanks to our embarrassing public school system in the United States, a full year to acclimate to a college environment and college-level work. We don't teach most athletes to learn; we teach them to hide, to cover up. And they learn it well. To keep them eligible we make them dependent on tutors and do not allow them the leisure to discover their own potential and become confident about their own ability to learn. Meeting their needs would take more time (and money) than we are willing to give them. It would take a freshman year without playing.

Second, stop pretending that anyone can play big-time college sports and carry the same academic load that regular students carry. Give the athletes a fifth year to finish school—with all the benefits received while playing. If the athlete goes pro, defer the fifth year and allow him to return when his professional career is over (sooner rather than later, in most cases). And while they are playing college ball, let them carry slightly lesser loads, so that they can concentrate on a few courses and learn something rather than take undemanding "jock" courses to fulfill unrealistic NCAA standards.

Do we do this? No. Instead we stuff them full of promises and dreams like so many Strasbourg geese. We expect too much of athletes—and too little of them. We demand extraordinary things of them on the field or court and less than ordinary things of them in the classroom. And, as with all self-fulfilling prophecies, the athletes come to define themselves within the contours of our lopsided expectations. It can be done the right way, there's no question about that, and Notre Dame is the perfect place to set the standards for all of college sports, to lead the way into a future in which the word *student-athlete* really means something, a future in which athletes can exploit their educational opportunities as much as we exploit the athletes. But instead of taking on this challenge, we peek through our fingers like children, looking at only the good parts of sports, snapping our fingers shut if anything unpleasant arises.

So much for my idle dreams. We opened the 1990–91 basketball season in the real world of unrealistic expectations. And to demonstrate that life has an ironic symmetry, our first game in this too-early NIT was against Fordham, the school that launched Dick's college coaching career. Frank and Susan McLaughlin came to South Bend for the game, Frank in his official capacity as Fordham athletic director and NIT official and Susan as his lovelywife. They invited us to dinner with them to catch up and reminisce. Dick and I go so far back with Frank that I feel as though we three grew up together, and in a way it's true. When Dick took the Fordham head coaching job in 1970, he hired

Frank, a twenty-three-year-old former Fordham player, as his assistant. Frank grew up in the Bronx and attended both Fordham Prep and the University. He knew the environs of Rose Hill like a gym rat. Then, when Dick jumped to Notre Dame after just a single year at Fordham, Frank went along. Still a bachelor and laden with Irish charm, Frank dated a succession of beautiful Notre Dame cheerleaders before settling on the stunning southern Susan Picton. Shortly after Susan and Frank were married, Frank left Notre Dame to become the head coach at Harvard. A few years later, he became Fordham's athletic director, the job for which he was made. Some people are lucky enough to end up in the perfect job for them—such is the fit between Frank and Fordham. I had to chuckle when I listened to him; he was having so much fun at his job. Yet even Frankie was aging: he was balding slightly, his face taking on that raw-boned look common to some Irishmen. But his humor was still irreverent and his eyes sparkled. During dinner at the Carriage House, I met Susan's eye and we shook our heads and laughed, wordlessly sharing our delight in Frank's forever-boyish pleasure in his position.

We easily defeated Fordham, playing with the eerie strains of the famous Fight Song coming from *outside* the arena. Because the basketball season began so early, it overlapped with football season and our Thursday night basketball game conflicted with the start of the Notre Dame–Penn State football weekend. The band could not play for the basketball team because it had to practice just outside the arena for its Saturday football performance. It was strange to hear the strains of the Fight Song filtering in through the walls, waking up the echoes for a phantom football crowd rather than for the real basketball crowd just yards away.

On Saturday night, after the football game (a loss to Penn State), we played the second round against Iowa before a somber crowd, without cheerleaders or a band. They were "too tired" from the football game to cheer us on. Luckily, playing in their absence was not completely unfamiliar. Frequently through the years, we played at NCAA tournament sites, the only team without band and cheerleaders—basketball, the stepchild sport at Notre Dame. Dick usually tried to round up a local high school band to play for the team on the road. Since many Catholic high schools had appropriated Notre Dame's Fight Song for their own, they knew how to play it—or at least approximate it. We heard many unusual versions. Once the hired band confused our Fight Song with Michigan's and played "Hail to the Victors" over and over with great enthusiasm. They doubtless wondered why we were less enthusiastic.

For the Iowa game Dick recruited a high school band even though we were playing in South Bend. Without cheerleaders and with a hardly identifiable Fight Song in the background, we defeated Iowa, looking strong and fast and promising. This coaching stuff wasn't so bad, after all. Secretly, I was doubly rejoicing because a trip to New York City over Thanksgiving meant that I would not have to cook Thanksgiving dinner. The last time I didn't cook the requisite turkey, I was in the hospital giving birth to Karen, who would turn twenty-five in a week. It wasn't that I minded, it's just nice to have a break every few decades.

Nearly every Thanksgiving I could remember, we entertained basketball players—all the way back to the years when Dick was an assistant coach at Penn. Jimmy Wolf, a Penn freshman whom Dick had recruited, was our first player-guest; then Corky Calhoun, whom we took with our babies to the Thanksgiving Day parade on Broad Street in Philadelphia and then to our tiny apartment for turkey dinner.

In the early years at Notre Dame, Shawna DiBiaso and I tried to gather all the players for dinner in one place—my house. We set up tables in every room and engaged a caterer to prepare the food. My kitchen could never have handled enough turkey, stuffing, potatoes, and pies for fifteen basketball players, even if Shawna and I were foolish enough to attempt it. But the catered gravy was often like wallpaper paste and the mashed potatoes were little but whipped powder and water. We decided to regroup and figure out another way of handling the dinner so that we could all eat some real food without abandoning the players, who could not go home because of practice, to the school cafeteria.

We decided on a plan that persists a decade and a half later: each assistant coach takes a few players, and Dick and I take the freshmen for Thanksgiving dinner. We can all easily entertain these smaller groups in our homes. Our family usually heads for the cottage for a long weekend, and Dick drives the players up on Thanksgiving Day after practice. One year I had an inspiration. I asked Dick's secretary, Dottie, to call each freshman player's mother and get the name of (and, if possible, the recipe for) a family specialty that they had each Thanksgiving. I would prepare these specialties and make the players feel particularly comfortable and welcome on their first Thanksgiving away from home.

Thanksgiving Day found me spending endless hours in the kitchen preparing sweet potato pie, oyster stuffing, and a strawberry Jell-O mold, in addition to the usual elaborate Thanksgiving fixings. Exhausted, I sat down to dinner and watched expectantly as the dishes were passed, waiting for the exclamations of surprise and joy. "Oyster stuffing! My favorite!" Nothing happened. I waited a little longer, and then unable to contain myself I turned to the player on my left and said, "How do you like the oyster stuffing?"

"Is that what it is? I thought it tasted a little funny."

"Your mother said it was your favorite Thanksgiving dish."

"She did? Well, I guess I like it okay."

Not easily defeated, I turned to the player on my right. "How about that sweet potato pie?"

"It's okay."

"But your mother. . . ." I let it go.

I modified my inspiration and now save myself hours in the kitchen. When we sit down to Thanksgiving dinner, I ask each person, players included, to share a special Thanksgiving memory. It works much better.

Thanksgiving 1990, compliments of Notre Dame basketball and the preseason NIT, someone else would serve me the turkey dinner. And I would watch the Macy's Thanksgiving Day Parade from my hotel room and maybe even ice-skate at Rockefeller Center. I turned my plans over in my mind as we rode after the Iowa game to Karen and Jamie's (my daughter and son-in-law's) house to celebrate the beginning of a new season.

After every home game, we usually gathered with some of our friends at the University Club on campus. I can't remember how this ritual began, but over time, like Topsy, it "just growed." The University Club is a one-story, flat-roofed building just off Notre Dame Avenue—two large parking lots and a football stadium away from the basketball arena. Sometimes after games I waited for Dick outside the locker room, immersed in the throng of autograph seekers, who brandished their programs in front of the emerging players still damp from their showers. "Are you somebody?" they would ask every tall man in the vicinity. Often, though, Dick had interviews in the press room or a meeting with his assistants after the game, so I stood around until the game crowd cleared, feeling a bit awkward when people consoled me after a loss or congratulated me after a victory (what did *I* do, after all?), and hitched a ride with Fred and Mary.

By the time that Mary, Fred, and I arrived at the Club, two pitchers of beer (one regular, one light; the light beer marked by a napkin around the pitcher's handle) would have materialized on the large round table. John Houck, now recovered from his near-fatal aneurysm (although still speaking in a raspy voice), regularly held court. Mary, his wife, sat quietly by, laughing for the hundredth time at John's jokes. "Mary's a saint," John said frequently. No one disagreed. Mary Houck (nee Dooley) is a "townie," as is her sister Brigid, Tex Dutile's wife. The "Dooley girls" (as we sometimes called them) grew up in our neighborhood, their father Notre Dame's first placement director, their mother an editor at Saint Mary's. Tex attended Notre Dame Law School and boarded with the then-widowed Kate Dooley, where he met Brigid. "Love at first sight," he claims.

"Not quite that quick," Brigid retorts.

Tex, illogically enough, is from Maine and teaches in the law school with me. He worked his way through law school by playing the piano in South Bend clubs. He plays by ear, can play *anything*, and more than willingly sits for hours at their house parties, playing and playing as the guests sing along. I never let the fact that I can't carry a tune deter me from singing heartily until the wee hours. (I specialize in show tunes and know all the words to *My Fair Lady* and *Camelot*—Mordred's song, "The Seven Deadly Virtues," and Eliza Doolittle's "Wouldn't It Be Luverly?" are my fortes.) Although Tex gladly indulges me, *his* specialty is Elvis Presley imitations—"I want you, I need you, I uh-uh-uh love you. . . ."

The University Club used to have a piano that Tex sometimes played. One night he entertained until well after 2 A.M. The piano disappeared shortly afterwards, but we're assured there's no connection.

Sharon Regan, whom John calls the "Gidget of the Geritol set" because of her bubbly manner and sometimes off-the-wall remarks, with her ex-marine husband Brian, and Dave Link, the law school dean, with his quietly intelligent wife Barbara, complete the circle of regulars. The postgame gathering gives Dick and me a place to get things back in perspective. These folks love Notre Dame sports well enough, but they don't make an idol of them. They love us more, and we know they are our friends, win or lose.

After the Iowa game, the group quit the University Club for Karen and Jamie's house. It was Jamie's birthday and Karen invited us all for cake (and champagne; after all, Dick and Mary were along). We sang "Happy Birthday" to Jamie and then "If I can make it there, I'll make it anywhere. It's up to you, New York, New York."

10

I woke up in the city that doesn't sleep. But I had slept long and well, a deep for-once dreamless sleep, penetrated only by the sounds of distant sirens. The night before, the Big Apple, in its inimitable fashion, welcomed our freshmen players, two from Indiana, one from Michigan, and one from Illinois, and none ever in New York City. After arriving at the Marriott Marquis, situated at Broadway and 45th Street, the freshmen, along with a couple of the team managers, ventured out into the city night to find something to eat. They walked west. Now the Marriott Marquis is conveniently located in the heart of the theater district, but one would not want to frequent the area west of it. The neighborhood soon becomes subsumed into the underbelly of the city, as our players quickly discovered. First encounter: "Hey, you guys. Come over here, see what I got. Watches, gold chains, all solid gold. Anything here is yours for fifty bucks."

Brooks Boyer moved closer to take a look. "Hey, fifty dollars for a Rolex. I can't believe it."

"Don't!" the worldly manager asserted and pulled Brooks away from the buy of a lifetime.

Second encounter: a man bundled up in a dark overcoat sidled up to the group. "My man," he said. "Have I got what you need tonight." He pulled a small plastic bag filled with white powder from his pocket. "It will make you so-o-o happy." Even our midwestern freshmen knew enough not to jump at that opportunity.

Third encounter: a rather skimpily dressed young woman glided up to the Ross twins. "Oh, two of you! And so tall."

Gee, they thought, people are really friendly here. Just like Indiana. Out loud, Joe Ross said, "We're basketball players. Notre Dame, you know."

"Oh, basketball players. Maybe you'd like to come with me for a while and play some other games. Just fifty dollars for the two of you."

A hat trick. Three New York happenings before they had traveled two blocks from the hotel. When they reported this amid gales of laughter from the more experienced players, they accused the team of staging their initiation to the big city. "You all just set this up, didn't you? You think we're midwestern hayseeds so you tried to shock us." No need, in New York, to set anything up. At least they weren't mugged.

Frank McLaughlin happily reigned over the NIT festivities: dinner at the Tavern on the Green, its trees filigreed with glittering Christmas lights; an evening at *Aspects of Love;* Thanksgiving brunch for the coaches and their families in his suite overlooking Broadway with its spectacular view of the huge inflated balloons for which the Macy's parade is famous. Unfortunately, I was one of the few from Notre Dame who could enjoy it. There were, after all, those games to play. Arkansas, Arizona, and Duke had also come to play, all highly ranked teams. We were the "Cinderella team," and when we met Arizona on Wednesday night, we played as if we wore ill-fitting glass slippers. It was no contest, and the

Madison Square Garden fans turned in a stellar performance.

"Where'd you get those guys, Digger?"

"Christ, the spread is only 11; you trying to kill me?"

I lost my cool when a fan, sloshing beer from a huge paper cup, bellied up to the rail behind me and my daughters. Karen had just told us she was pregnant, and I was feeling more protective than usual. "Notre Dame sucks; Notre Dame sucks," he screeched in our faces, pressing, it seemed to me, dangerously close. I grabbed the Carolina-blue-sleeved arm of the usher near me. "Get this guy out of here," I hissed. "He's drunk and he might hurt us." A few ushers gathered and escorted him away.

I had completely embarrassed my daughters. "Mom, you really overreacted," Karen immediately told me.

"I can't believe you, Mom," Jenny supported her sister. "What's wrong with you? The guy's just a fan. You should be used to it by now."

They were right, of course. Like referees, coaches' wives must not have "rabbit ears," responding to idle comments from the crowd. My face burned with shame and I looked cautiously around, wondering what people thought of me. No one was paying attention to me, thank God. No one noticed that I had momentarily lost control, let it get to me.

The Garden fans stayed in the game until the end as Arizona delivered the mugging the freshmen had escaped the night before on 45th Street. In the past I thought it odd that single foul shots received so much attention in a lopsided game. The fans would cheer or boo loudly when a player made a foul shot that changed the score from 85–70 to 85–71. This was real team loyalty! Then someone took me aside and explained the spread to me—how bettors pick a team to win by a certain point differential. A foul shot, while meaningless to the game's outcome, might mean he wins or loses a great deal of money. The spread has the effect of making the Garden fans attentive to the end, but also brutal if they're losing money. Such must have been the case that night,

(Left to right) Father Deviney, who hired Dick at St. Gabriel's High School, with Fathers Homer and Conboy—our poker playing circle in Hazleton.

St. Gabriel's team, Pennsylvania State Champions.

Heading off for Notre Dame.

Dick with his first Notre Dame coaching staff, Dick DiBiaso (left) and Frank McLaughlin (center).

Dick's mom waltzes with Father Conboy to celebrate the 1974 win over UCLA.

Orlando Woolridge gets a gag gift from Santa Claus; (left to right) Bill Laimbeer, Dick (Santa), Orlando Woolridge, Tracy Jackson, Stan Wilcox, Kelly Tripucka, and Rich Branning.

A team trip to Europe with (left to right) Bill Laimbeer, Rick, Dick, and Bill Hanzlik.

Al McGuire and Dick compare coaching strategies.

Butch Waxman makes a coaching point to Digger Phelps during the Providence win.

Dick clowns with Rick at
Final Four practice.

David Rivers.

Dick, Gerry Faust, and
Dick's mom.

300 wins!

David Rivers and Drazen
Petrovic, in Yugoslavia.

John Paxson, Ed O'Rourke,
and Dick on the beach
at the annual
Labor Day Party.

The annual ceremonial apple picking with (left to right) Rick, Matt Kilcullen, the Shumates (John, Brittany, Marilyn, and John, Jr.), Dick, and Boris Juric.

Our last team, Thanksgiving Day dinner.

Our Notre Dame prayer group gathers for Mass at the lake.

The new generation: (left to right) Jamie, Karen, Dillon, Jenny, Dick, and me.

and our humiliating 30-point loss to Arizona would have many of them hiding from their bookies. They made their displeasure clear.

I should have grown immune to crowd abuse after all these years; a kind of psychic numbing surely should have set in by now. A mere five days ago it seemed as though the season might even be fun at times. Small chance of that; the Garden ushers typically refused to let us wait for the team near the locker room and forced us to exit with the crowd to take our own chances on ever finding the team bus and our ride back to the hotel.

Thanksgiving morning dawned clear, crisp, the air filled with expectancy. New York was at its best, the streets celebrating the holiday as thousands gathered to watch the historic parade. Dick left right after breakfast for a morning practice at the Garden; Rick headed out to Queens to have Thanksgiving dinner with a friend from the University of Toledo; Karen and Jamie had already returned to Pennsylvania to spend the holiday with Jamie's parents. The official party traveling with the basketball team was sparse since the football team was playing on the West Coast against Southern California on the weekend. Anyone who was anyone at Notre Dame was catching pregame sunshine in Los Angeles. So Jenny and I ventured alone to the brunch for the coaches' families and NIT officials.

I was pleased to have some time alone with Jenny. She is our most enigmatic child, hard to read, always hesitant to let us know what she is thinking or feeling. These characteristics worried us particularly then. Jenny was a senior at Notre Dame, a student at the same place where her father was under so much pressure. When we asked her if that was hard on her, she always said no, that the disgruntled students were a small minority and she never, or seldom, ran into them. Still, she had entered little into the life of the school and lived off-campus with her roommates from her junior year.

Jenny was only two when we moved to South Bend, and she has no memories of any other home. She and her friend Kristin spent their childhoods exploring the campus, and Jenny sometimes came home with hair-raising tales of where they had been. They had once (going against all parental warnings) roller-skated through the underground tunnel that connects the Morris Inn to the Center for Continuing Education across the street; they had climbed to the very top of Washington Hall, searching for its fabled ghost (Knute Rockne's winter quarters, perhaps); they regularly waded or swam in the reflecting pool in front of the library mural. One such springtime plunge had captured the attention of a *South Bend Tribune* photographer: I picked up the evening Metro section to see Jenny's smiling wet face. At least no one had asked for her name. And these were the stories she told us. God only knows what else they did and judged unfit for our consumption.

Because of her familiarity with the campus, we were surprised when Jenny told us she wanted to go to Notre Dame. It would have been wiser for her to go elsewhere, get out of South Bend for a while, try something new. Now she was marooned on a campus where the climate had shifted against her dad. After she, Karen, and Rick wrote to the school paper, some students hung a sign in a tree across from her dorm; it said "You have to believe we must dump Digger," mocking Dick's oft-quoted "You have to believe." She stubbornly stood under the tree until two guys offered to help her take it down. These same two, more typical Notre Dame students I like to think, wrote her a letter a few days later, after the team had finally posted a big win. "We're thinking of you and your family," it said, "and hope you all hang in there." They signed it "The Sign Avengers." Nonetheless, she had to dread walking across campus when a "Dump Digger" T-shirt might appear around the next corner or a vicious banner unfurl from a dorm window. Although Jenny dismissed our concerns with a joke or a diversion, she had to complete her schooling at Notre Dame at the worst of times.

Karen also attended Notre Dame, four years earlier, but we always knew exactly what Karen was going through. Karen's "what-you-see-is-what-you-get" personality hides nothing and never minces words. Although people tend to think that Karen looks like me, beneath appearances she is most like her dad of all our children. She loves sports and absorbed its ethos like a sponge. She played Junior Olympic basketball, organizing and raising money for the teams herself. She captained her high school basketball team and played as her father had, with 90 percent desire and 10 percent talent. She dated a series of excellent athletes, including Tim Kempton, one of Dick's players. Her taste for athletes once prompted Rick to claim that Karen looked in the local paper to see who the "Athlete of the Week" was and called him up for a date. Kidding aside, at one time Karen had former boyfriends playing three professional sports: hockey, football, and basketball. This was after she had married a professional baseball player.

I was less than thrilled when Karen called me from Chicago the summer she was working as an intern at WGN Studio to tell me she was dating one of the Chicago Cubs. She had been working in the booth at Cubs games with announcers Harry Caray and Steve Stone, and they were determined to fix her up with a player. "Mom," she complained in an earlier conversation, "they're all married or too old. I wish Steve and Harry would just give it up. I'm not interested." Then Jamie Moyer came up from the minors as the new left-handed starter. Unmarried, a suitable twenty-three—Steve and Harry pounced. But I had heard about Cindy Garvey's widely published troubles; worse, I knew a little too much about the road lives of professional athletes. This was not what I wanted for my daughter. Besides, couldn't we get away from *sports* for once? Did it have to permeate everything we did?

Fortunately I had been a mother too long to give voice to these concerns, even if I had been foolish enough to think she would have listened to me. Jamie—solid, salt-of-the-earth, faithful Jamie—became my son-in-law in 1988. And I became a baseball fan, discovering that ERA meant something other than a possible constitutional amendment. Yet as I watched Karen suffer through Jamie's injuries and losses, as I watched her ride the roller coaster of emotions involved in being a professional athlete's wife, I wondered why she didn't run, screaming, away from a life in sports. She grew up with it; she should have known what she was getting into.

Rick, on the other hand, was developing into the writer I hoped I'd have. He, more than my girls, grew up around the players. He often walked or rode his bike over to basketball practice, more, we now surmise, to pester the players than to cheer them on. Once, when he was seven or eight, he picked up some clumps of snow from outside the arena and pelted the players when they were in the shower after a particularly grueling practice. They'd had enough. Digger's son or not, he wasn't going to get away with this. So John Shumate, Gary Brokaw, and Dwight Clay picked up all four feet of him, put him in a locker, and shut the door. Then they left the locker room. Rick screamed and pounded on the door to no avail until, only a few minutes later, a manager arrived and released him from his much-deserved imprisonment. To his credit, he never told us about it. We only found out years later when Gary and Shu were assistant coaches at Notre Dame and they, with the now grown-up Rick, told us the tale. Rick suffered no lasting effects—no lifelong claustrophobia or fear of locker rooms or anything like that. He did develop a healthy fear of pestering the players, especially of doing anything to them with the omnipresent South Bend snow.

Oh, yes, Rick was an athlete, too, playing a little of everything through junior high school and the early years of high school before concentrating on football, his first love. I didn't enjoy being a middle linebacker's mother, especially when Rick began to play at the University of Toledo and the opposing linemen outweighed him by fifty pounds. Finally, in his last year, Rick decided he'd had enough of sports on the field and turned to sports on the page. As sports editor of the college paper, he sent me copies of his columns. His childhood intimacy with and indifference to sports had developed into a sophisticated skepticism that was refreshing in a sports column. Pleased as I was that he escaped the football field without serious injury, I was having a little trouble adjusting to being the mother of a sportswriter, having always followed the lovelywife's motto: "Mothers, don't let your babies grow up to be sportswriters."

At the NIT brunch Jenny and I saw Frank and Susan's startlingly grown-up daughters. It seemed like yesterday that Frank introduced us to Susan after a Notre Dame basketball game. Susan was still glowing from the exertion of cheering and holding her pompoms at her side, her thick Texas accent drawling, "I'm pleased ta meet y'all." I immediately thought, Aha, this just might be the one.

Mike and Micki Krzyzewski were also at the brunch with their daughters yet we all seemed awkwardly to avoid each other. Mike had been rumored to be Dick's replacement at Notre Dame, although why on earth he would leave Duke escaped me. Nonetheless, the rumor made me feel ill at ease with them, unsure of what to say. They probably thought I was being aloof and standoffish. I don't like the way this year is changing me, I thought. Like last night at the Garden. I'm overreacting and suspicious.

Jenny, on the other hand, mixed easily and giggled as Frank told her how pretty she was. Frank was amazed that the funny toddler he knew had grown into a lovely woman. Jenny laughed at his teasing and moved around the room, carefree for this moment.

Dick and I had not told our children about the behind-the-scenes problems at Notre Dame. It has never been easy for them to grow up as "Digger's kids." They've met several presidents and have flown on private jets, but they've also had to contend with gossip and false friendships. Once, when Jenny was a freshman and Rick a sophomore at St. Joseph's High School, I heard a rumor that they were taking and selling drugs. "All the teachers at the high school know about it," I was told. One teacher had even talked about it to my informant. None of my "friends" who had heard the rumor had seen fit to tell me about it sooner. Rick and Jenny denied it and we had never seen anything in their behavior to indicate drug use. "Mom, people always talk, especially about us," Rick tried to reassure me. When Dick called home from his recruiting trip, we discussed what to do. "I don't believe it for a minute," I said, "but I don't want to be naive either."

"My God," he said. "Why do people have to talk about our kids?"

"This hurts more than anything anyone has ever said about us. I can't ignore it. I have to do something."

"I wish I could get home sooner. I'll cancel out on the last two recruits. I'll come home tomorrow."

"You can't do that. I can handle this."

The next morning, after a sleepless night, I called the high school principal, Glenn Rousey, and told him what I had heard. "If it's true, I have to do something about it," I nearly wept into the telephone. "If it's not true, I want to try to stop the talk." I asked for a meeting that day with the principal and with the teachers who had talked about it. Glenn made the arrangements and we met that afternoon: "I want to know," I began, "if Rick and Jenny are on drugs. If they are, I want to know why no one has bothered to tell me before now. Why did I have to hear this via some rumor mill?"

"Well, I just mentioned once that I was keeping an eye on them," one teacher said evasively.

"Then they're not on drugs?"

"Not that I know."

"Somebody must have misunderstood something I said," the other teacher said. "I don't think they're on drugs."

When the teachers left the room, I turned to the principal. "How could this happen? We've tried to protect them. We wanted them to be able to live normal lives in this town. This rumor about them is all over town. It's so unfair. It can ruin their lives."

"You and Digger have done a good job, Terry. They're great kids. Normal, down-to-earth. But I don't think you know what they go through. I watch them in the halls. I see kids dance around them, trying to be friends with them because of the coach. I see kids get on their cases after a loss. You can't protect them from everything. I'll talk to the teachers. I'll see to it that this particular rumor is stopped. But there will be others. It's the nature of things." He leaned toward me, "It's the nature of a town like this."

Jenny joined me at the window overlooking the parade and we watched Mighty Mouse come bobbing down Seventh Avenue. Below us the sidewalk vendors were hawking "cashmere" scarves and "gold" bracelets. Real, fantasy, fake, all mixed and difficult to decipher. "Let's go shopping on the street, let's go skating at Rockefeller Center," Jenny said. I reached out protectively and then withdrew my arm.

"Great idea. Let's go."

11

F our of us sat around the table—Jenny, Karen, Jamie, and I.
Dick was with the team, awaiting a game in Indianapolis; Rick
had returned to school at Toledo. I read aloud from the tattered
Advent book:

> Lord, Eternal God,
> come to us as we light the first candle
> and clear the darkness within us.
> Forgive the wrong we have done.
> Forgive us the good we could have done and never did.
> Teach us to wait and watch and recognize the
> coming of Christ
> in the needs we see around us,
> in the tasks he gives us to do.

Jenny leaned forward and lighted the purple candle in the Advent
wreath, as the rest of us sang an off-key version of "O Come, O

Come, Emmanuel." The candle glow in the darkened room engulfed us in a closed circle of wavering light. "Teach us to wait." This indeed would be a year of waiting: the joyful waiting for Karen and Jamie's baby; the disquieting waiting for the unseen shape of the end of the basketball season. We could see our future life only through a glass darkly and we prayed each to ourself that the darkness would be cleared away.

The NIT did not end badly. A consolation game is usually an emotional letdown for a team and an underdog has a decided advantage, more to prove. We got hot in the first half and had a shot at beating Duke, losing by only 8 points, a vast improvement over the 30-point margin against Arizona. Five days later back in South Bend, we nearly upset highly ranked Indiana. Indiana had played in a Thanksgiving tournament in Hawaii and had just returned the day before. They showed up in South Bend with a case of near-terminal jet lag. The arena was packed with as many red shirts showing as blue and gold. Indiana missed shots and offensive rebounds, so we could run and press: it's basic in basketball—to play a running game, you need to have the ball. Unfortunately, the Indiana team managed to shake off some of its fatigue in the second half and our intensity lessened in the final ten minutes. We lost by 3.

But yesterday's game against Kentucky dealt us a second mortal blow. We were playing in the Hoosier Classic, in which Indiana, Kentucky, Louisville, and Notre Dame played a doubleheader each year. The fact that these teams were coached by four of the most colorful, and controversial, coaches in the business— Bobby Knight, Rick Pitino, Denny Crum, and Digger Phelps— made the Hoosier Classic a stellar attraction, drawing as many as 45,000 fans to the Hoosier Dome in Indianapolis.

Denny Crum was working under particular pressure. "60 Minutes" had recently run an unflattering portrait, an exposé really, about his basketball program at Louisville. When it was revealed that thirty-one of the thirty-nine players who had played for him failed to graduate, he got defensive and responded that at least those players had gotten a chance to play and perhaps make it to the pros. The new president at the University of Louisville apparently was not pleased with his university functioning as a farm club for professional basketball and demanded that changes be made. Denny will find, as we have, that it's not easy to do both, graduate players and win enough games, year after year, to please the fans.

Rick Pitino, wonder boy of the early nineties, had just arrived at Kentucky to rescue its celebrated basketball program from the misdeeds of the past. In Kentucky, basketball ranks just behind horse racing and far ahead of any other religion. For years we had played Kentucky right after Christmas, at a "neutral" site—Louisville. Kentucky fans made an annual pilgrimage for the game and the air in Freedom Hall was filled with the soft scent of bourbon and the continual chant "Go Blu-ue." Because the game occurred over the Christmas holidays, we often made the game a family trip, and in Louisville my children first experienced having to hear strangers say bad things about their father. My children would spend some of the day riding the elevators in the Executive Inn where we stayed with the team, and where many of the Kentucky fans also put up for the pilgrimage. In packed elevators the blue-clad Kentucky devotees would loudly disparage Notre Dame, its basketball team, its coach, anything Irish and everything Catholic. When Jenny complained to me about it, I told her to speak up. In the crowded elevator between floors when the jibes started, she should just perk up with "Digger Phelps is my *Daddy!*" Giggling to myself, I played out the ensuing scene in my mind, imagining little Jenny innocently lisping out the words and the shocked looks on the fans' faces.

It was also during a hotly contested Kentucky game that Rick best demonstrated his then-characteristic ennui. Dick always let Rick sit on the bench; friends around the country watched Rick grow up on TV. This particular year he was ten, sitting in the row just behind the team along with the trainer and team doctor. It was a crucial game with the winner poised to move into the number-one spot in the rankings. Thirty seconds remained in the game and Notre Dame trailed by a single point with the ball. Rick leaned forward and tapped his father's shoulder: "Dad, could I have a quarter to get a Coke?" I had tried to teach my children to keep the games in perspective. Perhaps I had gone too far?

But Kentucky basketball fell on hard times a few years ago when $1,000 spilled out of an Emery Express package going to a recruit. While it didn't surprise those of us in the game—rumors of Kentucky's creative recruiting had been around for as long as I could remember—it did surprise the NCAA. The subsequent investigation generated stories, some never substantiated, of irregularities, including a recruit's cheating on the SATs. The NCAA found enough to justify a two-year probationary period in which the Kentucky basketball team could neither appear on television nor play in postseason tournaments. The coach, Eddie Sutton, resigned, took a year off, and then assumed the head coaching job at Oklahoma State. Exit Eddie Sutton. Enter Rick Pitino, hot off the Knicks, hot off Providence College. Smart enough not to stay too long in one place.

And then there's Teflon Bobby Knight, one of the most complicated men I've ever known. On the one hand, there's the private Bobby—generous, soft-hearted, a good listener, my friend. On the other hand, there's the public Bobby, whose outrageous acts I need not reopen here. I know he's really the private person, the man with whom I would trust nearly anything. I wish he'd let the public in on that guy. But, then again, why should he? Bobby gets away with anything. No one, *no one* else would have lasted as long as he has behaving the way he sometimes does. His public acts just wash right off.

And Digger Phelps—once wonder boy like Rick Pitino; often of a dual public/private nature like Bobby Knight; and now working under pressure, for very different reasons, like Denny

Crum. Hard to imagine these four men in a single building. It takes one as large as the Hoosier Dome to contain them.

During yesterday's game against Kentucky, the team began to jell in the way it had been promising to for weeks. We were ahead by 7 shortly before the half when our senior point guard, Tim Singleton, dribbling near half court, suddenly went down as if he were shot in the back. He could neither get up nor return to the game and Kentucky went ahead to win by 8. Tim was diagnosed with a bulging disk in his lower back that would prevent him from playing for a minimum of six weeks.

We were now without Monty and without Tim, two starters, and, at the same time, confronting a major dilemma in negotiations with the University. Dick received a letter a few weeks earlier from Father Beauchamp, which begrudgingly said that they would allow Dick to coach one more year, *if* (among other things) he took a salary cut of over $20,000; he announced he would be leaving at the end of this year; and he cleared all recruiting decisions through the athletic director. As much as Dick wanted to fulfill his promise to his current players and coach them through their senior year, he found these conditions not only condescending but also difficult to implement. Having a lame duck coach in their crucial senior year was unfair to the seniors; the media attention would be focused on him and on speculation about his replacement. Rumors about his successor were already widespread. Would it be Pete Gillen, a former assistant now at Xavier? Mike Krzyzewski of Duke? P. J. Carlesimmo, whom Dick coached at Fordham, now at Seton Hall? And the way that Notre Dame had always recruited, finding out about a potential player's character and attitude, as well as about his grades and playing ability, was a complicated process. The Notre Dame basketball program had developed a strong and positive relationship with the admissions office (not a commonplace occurrence on most campuses) because of the willingness to screen potential student-athletes carefully before presenting them to admissions. If Rosenthal wanted to participate throughout the process, that was fine. But it didn't seem fair to let him step in at the end to veto or approve a recruit, basing his decision on abstract statistics or on one of the national "rating" services that ranked high school prospects. Dick was working on a letter trying to explain his position, in between preparing for Indiana and Kentucky. The strain was showing; a plot to break his concentration could not have worked better.

Typically Dick buried himself in videotapes to prepare for a game. If he had his preferred three days to prepare, he would outline strategies the first day and then build the intensity during the subsequent practices. He and his assistants, working in the "war room," a room equipped with video screens, blackboards, and architect-style desks, would watch three selected games that the upcoming opponent had played, winding and rewinding the tapes, breaking plays down into their component parts and preparing offenses or defenses to match up to them. One assistant was assigned to a particular game and was responsible for selecting the tapes and for doing preliminary work: putting together a fifteen-minute "highlight" tape of the opponent and a fifteen-minute "game-flow" tape. They would show five to ten minutes of these tapes to the Notre Dame team before the first preparatory practice so that the players would begin to get a feel for the upcoming opponent. Dick also included some film of how the opponent played at the end of a game; innumerable games were won or lost in the final thirty seconds. In the war room, Dick would analyze the three complete game tapes with all his assistants and bounce ideas off them. He looked for what he called "wrinkles": little things that a powerful opponent did not do well—blocking out, for example. Then he prepared his "game cards": 4 × 6 index cards that listed wrinkles, plays, options, defenses, offenses. He revised the cards after practices and had the final version ready for the game. Notre Dame's playing strategy not only had to counter the opponent's strengths and weaknesses, but also capitalize on what our players could do and circumvent what they couldn't.

The University of Nevada at Las Vegas style run-and-gun had become the rage and our fans frequently became impatient with Dick's more deliberate, taking the time to set up, offenses. So did I at times, enjoying as much as anyone the flashy play, the slam dunk, the alley-oop. But I had also seen what could happen if we tried to run with a team such as Arizona that was loaded with talent—faster, bigger, stronger, more accurate. We couldn't compete. If a team has more talent, if they're better at run-and-shoot, the advantage immediately goes to them. In those cases, Dick tried to figure out how to keep it close for 39 minutes and then "steal" the game at the end. Our players had to play smarter, think more, overcome deficiencies with strategy. Dick believed in playing with a purpose and forcing an opponent to play *his* game: multiple offenses and defenses. He believed in doing whatever they had to do to win the game. Sometimes it even worked and we won games when we were clearly outmanned. Sometimes it didn't, and the fans screamed for a more exciting style of play. "I'd love to play run-and-shoot," Dick often said to me. "We just never have five guys that talented so we can. Maybe someday."

So he watched tapes and moved his X's and O's around like chessmen, looking for a weakness here, an opening there. And he worked on his letter to Father Beauchamp, trying to figure out how to articulate, to someone who didn't want to listen, what the basketball program meant to him. He finally mailed it just before leaving for the UCLA game on the West Coast.

The Notre Dame–UCLA series goes back at least three decades. When we first arrived at Notre Dame, UCLA was somewhere in the middle of its 88-game winning streak and was the perennial NCAA champion. In Dick's first game coaching against them, we lost 114–56, the same year we lost to Indiana by 65. He narrowed the gap in 1973 and set the stage for the stunning upset in 1974.

We were enduring an unusually bad patch in our marriage. I had graduated from Notre Dame in August and continued right on to graduate school. Although Dick always agreed that I should finish college, the idea of my being in school for several more years surprised and unnerved him. Graduate school was not in my original plans, but my return to school so enlivened me that I didn't want it to end. I felt reaffirmed, close to establishing an identity of my own. I was, admittedly, somewhat obsessed with school, in love with talk and ideas. It distracted me from the difficulties I felt in being a lovelywife; it gave me a place where I was comfortable, a place that I quickly embraced.

At the same time, Dick's star was on the rise. The year before, only his second at Notre Dame, the team had come close to winning the NIT, losing to Virginia Tech in the final seconds. The team's quick success, and its young, colorful coach, galvanized the fans. It also put Dick on the road to fame. A *Sports Illustrated* writer, Larry Keith, contacted Dick about doing a book about him and about the season, and when Dick agreed, Larry practically moved to town. I liked Larry well enough, but with him constantly underfoot I felt that my life had become material for a sports book: *A Coach's World* with me playing a bit part, reduced to lovelywife status. More than ever, I felt pressure in trying to figure out how one went about being a coach's wife. How could I possibly do it? I felt doomed to failure. Then in the middle of January, UCLA, victorious in 88 straight games, came to town.

At the close of practice the day before the game, Dick made the players practice cutting down the nets. Dick's assistants as well as the players thought that Dick had finally gone off the deep end. They hoped the game would be close, but *win?* Come on.

The last 3 minutes and 21 seconds of that game are permanently engraved in my brain, not only because it was truly a memorable win but also because it was a kind of watershed in my life as a coach's wife. After the game, the phone rang constantly for days. Telegrams poured in from people, some long-forgotten former "roommates" or "fraternity brothers." Dick became a big story. I had married Dick Phelps, and I really didn't mind this

"Digger Phelps" public persona as long as it stayed in the public arena. But Digger Phelps, it seemed, was now the person with whom I lived. I retreated more and more into my books. Somewhere in them, I thought, I would find out how to live a real life. The winning was unquestionably heady. But it was also for me finally empty. This was *it?*, I wondered. People cared too much about a game. Perhaps it stood for something else, was a metaphor for some other more significant victory. I turned to my books to find the answer. Above all I felt intensely lonely. It seemed as if everyone understood something that I could not. I only knew that we were on the fast track, the slippery slope to God-knows-where. And I wanted off.

The differences between Dick and me—and they were always considerable—became more pronounced. Day and night, fire and ice, we've been described. Dick took to celebrity like a duck to water. He drove a blue-and-gold Thunderbird (on loan from a local car dealer), dressed in the latest fashion (or fad), hobnobbed with the rich, famous, and powerful. He was a natural. I, on the other hand, was no duck in this water. I preferred puzzling over the intricacies of *Paradise Lost* with my graduate student friends or writing poetry of my own. My idea of a good time was to stay at home with a book. The more of a celebrity Dick became, the more I fought it. He was the master of hyperbole, I of understatement or no words at all. His life was purposeful; he always seemed to know where he was going and why—a knight on a Grail quest. I was serendipitous, adaptive, spontaneous; I let things happen and then worked them out. I hated stylish clothes and refused to buy them, so Dick returned from trips with plenty of gifts for me—all clothes. I gave him books for Christmas and dragged him to concerts and art galleries. "There's a world outside of basketball!" I constantly insisted. "Sports just aren't that important. There are politics and art and literature, all kinds of things." After a while, he listened, probably because I never let up. He broadened his interests; it made him a better person and, I sometimes think, a less effective coach, although I doubt that he would see it that way. If he cared more about the world and less about winning, his intensity was surely undermined.

It was a strain for me to be the object of attention. I felt invaded, studied like a bug on a pin. Dick reveled in it and became accustomed to being the focus of media and public scrutiny. I discovered things about him I never had known—how, for example, he loves being the center of attention. "Does he bring it home?" people ask, referring to the pain of a loss. Never. He only brings home needing to be the center of attention.

But you get used to being special, not standing in line for anything, not needing reservations, receiving special favors. I tried to stay above it all, with limited success. "It annoys me when people treat you different," I'd say repeatedly. "You're just an ordinary person." Then one night Dick and I were driving home after an evening in Chicago and Dick asked me to take over the wheel for the last endless stretch from LaPorte to South Bend, twenty-six miles that feel like a hundred. He promptly fell asleep in the passenger seat. After a short while I saw red lights flashing behind us and realized that I was too anxious to get home—about ten miles an hour too anxious. The state trooper flashed his light in my face. "License and registration, please." I reached for my wallet and Dick stirred.

"What's going on?" The flashlight beam shifted to his face.

"Coach Phelps! How're you doing? Great game against Marquette!" The trooper stopped long enough to glance at my license. "Now, Mrs. Phelps, I'm not going to give you a ticket, but you slow down. Watch that speed limit, okay?"

He walked away and I rolled up the window. Dick was fully awake by now. "Go on, Terry. Tell him you *want* that ticket. No special favors for you, right?" I glared at him, started the car, and set the cruise control for fifty-five.

You get used to special favors. You get used to staying in suites, getting picked up by limousines, and flying in private jets.

You get used to meeting presidents—of corporations and countries. You become dependent on largesse and that comes with a price. Wherever you go, all the time, you're the coach and his lovelywife.

Celebrity is a strange beast, coming at first as a friend, welcomed, desired. Then just as it seems to become domesticated, part of the family, it transforms, subtly turns on you. It begins to take up more room, to demand more space. There's nowhere you can go without it, it intrudes into the most private places. You begin to wonder why you ever wanted it in the first place, but it's too late. It has insinuated itself into your life and will not go away. For me, Dick's new celebrity status lived with us like a distant cousin who comes to stay and won't go home; for Dick, I think, it was more like a mistress—he became infatuated and unaware of its danger to our family and our relationship.

We could go nowhere without Dick being recognized and asked for autographs or given advice on how to win more games. We stopped going to restaurants because we rarely got through a meal without someone approaching Dick and saying, "I shouldn't interrupt you but . . ." I planned a trip to Europe hoping for some privacy but someone recognized Dick as we walked along the Champs Elysée. Finally we planned backpacking trips with the children. In the wilds of Colorado, Wyoming, and Vancouver Island we could have fun together without the world looking on.

In the 1990–91 season we played UCLA just once, in Pauley Pavilion on UCLA's campus. On my single trip there with the team a few years earlier, Westwood and the UCLA campus seemed like something out of a fairy tale. Bougainvillea spilling over walls, leggy girls in shorts and halter tops walking about in the warm sunshine, god-like young men, tanned, riding skateboards. No wonder they had managed to dominate college basketball for so long. Who wouldn't want to go to school there?

UCLA basketball had lost some of its luster, on its sixth coach since John Wooden retired in 1975. Still, perhaps because of his many notable victories there, Pauley was Dick's absolutely favorite place to play. The fans, who frequently arrived hours before the game, screamed at him: "Digger's a wimp! Digger's a wimp!" Dick cupped his hand to his ear: "Louder. I can't hear you," he yelled back. The crowd took up the challenge. "Digger's a wimp!" filled Pauley Pavilion. Dick waved and bowed majestically. These games were equal parts Hollywood and sports. Dick was truly the center of attention, getting to play his favorite role, and he loved it.

I forwent the 1990 trip under the pressure of grading 180 writing papers from my Legal Writing course, as well as papers from my new course, Gender Issues in the Law. December was always a difficult month for me as I juggled finishing up the semester, preparing for Christmas, and surviving the pressures of an incipient basketball season. December is when I am most likely to fold under with fatigue and other MS symptoms.

It was also the time when Dick and his assistants began to sweat out the players' grades and their eligibility for the second semester. Notre Dame has one of the strictest eligibility requirements of all NCAA schools. The NCAA has a hands-off policy: whatever a school establishes for eligibility in general applies to its athletes as well. At Notre Dame, a student has to maintain a 2.0 average each semester to be eligible to participate in sports. Because basketball spans two semesters, the players have to get a 2.0 average the first semester or they are ineligible to play for the rest of the year. They do not have a buffer semester to bring up their grades as do the football players. And Notre Dame has no "Recreation" major in which athletes can hide.

Nearly every player thinks he is in great shape in a course until finals roll around. Like typical students, they put off worrying until the last minute, which means that everyone else has plenty of worrying to do. LaPhonso, on whom so much depended that year, especially since we'd lost Monty and Tim, had already been ineligible for the first semester of his sophomore year. He was an accouting major and first-semester junior year is deadly for many accounting majors, athletes or not. Losing LaPhonso to grades was the last thing we needed then.

We lost successively to the state of California: by 8 to UCLA out there and by 10 to Southern Cal at home the night before exams began. Southern Cal's coach, George Raveling, is a good friend, and whatever the game's outcome, we were happy to be able to spend some time with him. George spent part of his childhood in a boys' home in Pennsylvania and was recruited to play at Villanova. A great basketball player, he used the sport wisely, becoming educated, sophisticated, worldly, urbane. For us, he's a wonderful model for our players; basketball is a means to an end, not the end itself. He too was coaching basketball at a football school, and George, no fool, kept his options open. He was a likely candidate to replace Joe VanCisin, the president of the National Association of Basketball Coaches. Dick was campaigning for him behind the scenes, and they compared notes and political strategies after the game.

We had now lost seven games in a row and in the face of "No comment" from the Notre Dame administration, the national press speculated about Dick's future at Notre Dame. Silence makes a strong statement, and many sportswriters took a cynical view of Notre Dame's failure to support a long-time coach. In mid-December, Malcolm Moran's *New York Times* column carried the headline "Notre Dame's Digger: Victim of Hypocrites." It read: "In the basketball court of public opinion, Phelps is becoming the victim of the type of hypocritical thought he has fought most of his professional life. The recent criticism that has engulfed his program, despite his athletes' superior graduation rate, his Notre Dame record of 383–184 and 14 appearances in the National Collegiate Athletic Association tournament, including the last six seasons, has created the most recent unflattering example of the state of college athletics. In an era of purported enlightenment, the unhappiness in the stands at Notre Dame suggests that in the minds of too many people who watch these games, the degrees earned by all 54 Irish players who have competed for four years under Phelps are nothing more than window dressing, a far less significant statistic than the score of the most recent game." One of my colleagues, a priest, posted the article on a bulletin board outside our faculty offices, in the common space that he and I shared. It was one of the last things I saw each day as I left the law building and its headline rang like a mantra as I walked the mile home.

We had a ten-day break between games as the players took time off from basketball and prepared for their first-semester exams. They tried like most students to pull it all together at the end. Dick even made practice optional and some days graduate assistant Jim Dolan had to suit up so that there were enough players for a scrimmage. Not playing over exams was a crucial University policy that seemed to be in some jeopardy two years ago after Dick lost control of scheduling decisions. But the University provost and the Faculty Board in Control of Athletics (a misnomer if I ever heard one—the dean of the law school, Dave Link, was on the board for years and he used to joke about how the board got to approve the schedule: "This year we approved the two-inch by three-inch size," he'd say) actually noticed and stepped in. We still played over exams that year, but it was made quite clear that it was never to happen again. Dick was relieved that the burden of protecting the players academically was shared.

Dick used the break to prepare for his most important yearly game: the Christmas party game at Logan Center, a local school for the mentally disabled. Our first year in South Bend, now twenty years ago, Dick first played in the basketball game against Logan Center that preceded its annual Christmas party. Every year since then Dick has rounded up his assistants, other coaches, neighbors, and family (Rick played as soon as he was old enough;

Jamie married into the game) to constitute his team. Opposing them has been the Logan Center team, composed of the Center's present and former students, captained by Irving "Butch" Waxman, player-coach extraordinaire. The end of each year's game was the same. Logan Center was up by 1; Butch had effectively shut down scoring ace Digger "What, *Me* Pass?" Phelps. With seconds remaining in the game, Phelps dribbled down the floor, confident in his ability to sink the winning basket. The crowd was on its feet, most of them cheering for Logan Center, the rest (the Notre Dame basketball players) cheering for Digger's team because they had to. With a second left, Phelps paused, set up, and shot, with Butch "In Your Face" Waxman sticking to him like Velcro. The ball bounced hard off the rim, hung for a heartbreaking instant above it, and fell away. Logan Center won again and Butch and the boys were jubilant.

Despite Dick's annual humiliation at the hands of Butch Waxman, they became friends. Butch pulled no punches and readily told Dick what he thought of his coaching. One year the team had just lost to Maryland on the road and was playing Providence College at home. At the half Notre Dame was down by 6. Butch and his friend Tommy, with a social worker in tow, showed up during halftime in the locker room. Butch was one of the few people who had invariable access to the locker room. Butch yelled at Dick and told him that his game plan at Maryland stunk. "Don't yell at me, yell at the players," Dick replied and gestured toward the team sitting on benches in front of a blackboard covered with X's and O's. So Butch did, and he turned to the blackboard to adjust the game plan against Providence. "It worried me a little," Dick told me later, "when Kempton and Barlow followed along closely and nodded in agreement."

When the team returned to the floor, Butch lingered by the bench. The referees whistled for the game to recommence and Dick looked around for the social worker to take Butch back to his seat. The social worker had disappeared. "Sit in my seat," Dick told Butch quickly, not wanting to risk a technical foul for delaying the jump ball. Dick always squatted near the bench during the games, so his seat was vacant and available for Butch. Notre Dame started fast and finally went ahead with its momentum building. Dick heard someone yelling behind him, "Time out, time out!" Dick spun around and glared at his assistants—Gary Brokaw, Jim Baron, and Peter Gillen—"What the hell, Peter!" on his lips.

"It's not me, Coach," frenetic assistant Gillen protested. "It's *Butch.*" Dick had completely forgotten that Butch was sitting on the bench.

"I want to talk to the players," Butch explained.

"Not now, Butch. There's a TV time-out in 30 seconds and you can talk to them then." Dick's patience with Butch was endless. Fortunately the social worker reappeared (at Peter's bidding) and escorted Butch to his seat in the stands. Notre Dame held on to the lead and won.

In 1990 the Logan Center game was scheduled, as always, two Sundays before Christmas. It was the first thing Dick wrote in his calendar every year and nothing interfered with it. The game progressed as usual, with Digger's team keeping it close. There were a few seconds left and Logan Center was predictably ahead by 2 points. Jamie "Was *This* in the Marriage Contract?" Moyer dutifully passed to his father-in-law. Digger dribbled down the court; Butch was guarding him. A second was left, Digger shot and would miss as usual. The ball bounced, hung, and fell through the rim! No one could believe it. The crowd was silent; Butch and his team were paralyzed, their heads turned toward the basket, unable to believe that they saw the shot hit. For a moment they thought they had lost; then they realized that the score was tied and regrouped for the overtime. Digger's team, having come so close for once, was too tired and Logan Center dominated the overtime and won by 5.

Dick has learned a great deal from his friend Butch Waxman. Mrs. Waxman told us that when Butch was a baby she was informed that he would never be able to do anything for himself:

not even feed or dress himself. With the help of Logan Center, Butch developed far beyond the doctors' bleak prediction. As an adult, he could ride a bus to work and lived in a group home. He was a functioning and contributing member of the community and Dick saw him as a perfect example of his "You have to believe" philosophy. Because of Butch's influence and friendship, Dick served on Logan Center's Protective Services Board and fretted constantly about the Center's financial situation. And he made group homes his special interest.

"Take a study break," my invitation to my seminar students and teaching assistants read. "Stop by and help us trim our tree. Pizza and Christmas cheer provided." Dick invited the players and they, with my students, made short work of trimming our immense tree. Unlike most trees, the *top* of our tree was more fully decorated, the players having had little difficulty reaching the uppermost branches.

Two of my students, Garth and Leisle, were lawyers from South Africa at Notre Dame to do graduate work on human rights and the law. They brought a refreshing and sometimes startling perspective to the Gender Issues course and helped the rest of the class see how sex discrimination operated in their culture, in which discrimination was the order of the day. Their presence that night with Dick's players made me remember the wonderful power of sports, in which differences are leveled in an open and healthy competition. Sports has the ability to bring all sorts of people together, to give them something in common, something to share. It can be a singular bridge linking disparate cultures, transcending politics, erasing borders. Teach me to wait, I thought as I watched the players devour pizza, cookies, and punch, occasionally decorating each other with some tinsel, acting like the kids they were, ribbing each other. I lighted the Advent wreath and silently mouthed the words again: "Teach us to recognize the coming of Christ in the needs we see around us, in the tasks he gives us to do."

12

December 20 brought Dick's parents visiting from New York for Christmas and a return letter from Father Beauchamp. "The offer to allow you to continue coaching the basketball season for the 1991–92 season is *withdrawn*," the underlining gratuitously calling attention to the wielding of raw power. "Certainly, it is the University's hope that you will be willing to announce that you have decided to resign as the head basketball coach at Notre Dame. However, if you choose not to do so, there will be an announcement made by the University that a decision has been made to terminate your coaching responsibilities."

"I guess he doesn't read the *New York Times*," I said when Dick showed it to me. But he did not laugh on cue.

"I questioned some conditions so I'm finished. That's that," his face betraying the pain he felt. "I guess they'll fire me. I can't see myself lying about this and resigning. What an ugly feeling."

"What can I do?"

"Nothing. Let's just get through Christmas as best we can. Don't say anything to the kids or my parents about this. Meanwhile I've got to figure out a way to get this team to regroup without Timmy. We really don't have a true point guard without him."

"Do you think they'll actually have the nerve to fire you? After all the bad publicity they've had lately? I'd think the national press would take them apart."

"Who knows? There's no way of knowing how they make decisions around here anymore. They don't seem to care much about public opinion."

"I still say fight it." My fighter-pilot hackles were up. "They think they know so much about basketball. They have all the answers. Make them take a stand."

"Getting fired isn't much fun, but there's nothing else to do. God, what an empty feeling!"

My anger had so dissipated that I could not even call it forth. Instead I felt sick at heart and for the first (and only) time cried when I talked to one of my friends at work, a priest. "Why now?" I asked him. "This couldn't have waited until after Christmas? Or even after the season? What's the point?"

"I don't know what to tell you, Terry." He raised his hands in a gesture of helplessness and I was sorry that I cried in front of him and made him uncomfortable. "I don't think it's conscious cruelty. Just ineptness, not thinking about people's feelings. You know how I feel about Digger. He's perfect for Notre Dame. He stands for everything important to us. It's a mistake, but there's nothing anyone can do."

"I know. I know there's nothing you can do. I didn't come to ask you to try and change anything. I need to talk to someone; I need to understand. It makes no sense to me. I never expected Notre Dame to be this way."

"I'm afraid we priests are all too human. We make mistakes. Some of us aren't even necessarily nice people."

I stood to leave, gripped by the irony of where else could I have had such a conversation with such a friend? Where else would I have become so vulnerable and hence so wounded?

"I'm sorry. I shouldn't have dumped all this on you. It's just that I'm trying to be strong for Dick, for the kids, for everybody, and I don't feel very strong right now. I only feel overwhelmingly sad, beaten down, tired. I wanted Christmas to be a happy time and I can't seem to make that happen."

Exams were over and the basketball season resumed with a home game against Portland. Portland University, in Portland, Oregon, was not the type of team we usually had on our schedule. Because it is a sister school to Notre Dame, also run by priests of the Holy Cross order, we played them nearly every year. To my mind, it was a good idea. Things are at stake other than a power rating in composing a schedule. It's nice to give teams like Portland an opportunity to play here, a chance to play a team of Notre Dame's caliber. It would be too bad if we got so high and mighty, so far above the crowd, that we couldn't play teams like Portland anymore. That was the current fate of all the Ivy League schools we used to play—just not tough enough for us, according to the new regime.

I sent my in-laws off to the game with Rick and Jenny and finished preparations for our postgame pre-Christmas party. I expected over a hundred people so I skipped the game, a concession I'd made only lately. In past years when I hosted as many as five postgame parties during the season, I would attend the game and rush home afterwards, seconds before the first guests arrived. And I never used a caterer; not bragging, just confessing my stupidity.

When I first arrived at Notre Dame, scared silly at what one does as a coach's wife, Katie Parseghian, wife of then-football coach Ara Parseghian, was my model. The Parseghians had parties at their house after every home football game. They were laid back, comfortable affairs, with plenty of food that Katie had prepared herself. I even learned to eat *krema*, an Armenian concoction made of raw meat and bulgur. Having put Ara on a pedestal before we arrived at Notre Dame, we felt privileged to be part of the postgame crowd back at their house. And I wanted to be just like Katie. The only thing that I found a little strange was that Katie never went to the football games. "How could she stay away from all that excitement?" I wondered innocently.

I'm sure that Ara and Katie have no idea to what extent they served as role models for both of us, but we were lucky to have them there. Knowing them up close revealed no clay feet, just normal (albeit intense, in Ara's case) folks who happened to work at Notre Dame. From Katie, I thus adopted the practice of entertaining at home after games, instead of taking the easier, and probably wiser, course of renting space elsewhere. Sometimes I rue that training and wonder why I just don't put on a pretty dress and show up somewhere else—the perfect hostess. Instead I labor over crab dip, cut up vegetables, and, yes, even make a slightly English version of *krema*. I fuss with Christmas decorations and worry about having enough ice.

"Whatever way the ball bounces" read my invitation for our first big party in 1971. I invited everyone in the athletic department; we were a family then, sojourners in a common enterprise, working toward the same goal—integrating athletics into a great Catholic university. In addition to the athletic department, I invited everyone else I could think of: most of the English department, other faculty, Campus Ministry staff, name it. Being a basketball fan, or even a sports fan, was definitely not a requirement. In fact, some people called to find out what time the game would be over, so that they would know what "postgame" meant.

Less simple all these years later. The athletic department had grown tremendously in size and there were people who came and went whom I never even met. If there ever was a common enterprise, it was gone. The different sports seemed to have their own little groups, shut off from each other and that saddened me. Happily, even twenty years later, today's guests included the track coach, the lacrosse coach, and others whom we met all those years ago. And I still added people to the party list, throwing together deans and athletic trainers, priests and television anchorwomen, my neighbors and the assistant coaches.

I suppose it would have been easier, especially now, if we had simply treated Notre Dame basketball as Dick's job. "Just off to the office, dear. See you in the evening." But we didn't. It was a way of life for us and entered everything we did. I knew that it was not ordained to be so, but when I look back on that girl who shines out from a picture taken shortly after we arrived, I see unmitigated idealism. She sits in bell-bottoms and platform shoes with her arms around her children, leaning against her husband, her smile untroubled.

After the fabled UCLA victory, I began to realize that our life would not be untroubled, that the halcyon existence I had imagined as part of a college community was not to be. Dick had become *somebody*, the process that began at Fordham was now complete, and I, by virtue of being his wife, assumed a public status that I had not anticipated. What we did was of public interest, and when he sometimes picked me up from the library to take me to lunch—he so recognizable and me, in jeans, not looking much like the imagined Digger's wife—we generated rumors about "Digger and some blond." Everything we did seemed to whet the appetites of local gossips.

Perhaps worse than that, pressure to win also arrived with the UCLA victory. Before that game, Notre Dame basketball was not really a nationally recognized program. Notre Dame basketball fans, a select loyal few, were thrilled with wins and complacent about defeats. It was a game safely hiding in football's shadow at Notre Dame. No more. Nationally the program began to rank among the best in the country. New "fans" arrived. Like Dr. Frankenstein, Dick had unknowingly created something he could not control. The bandwagon brought fans with expectations: losing was not tolerated, winning by too few points was not acceptable. Win and win big—all the time—or damned near if you knew what was good for you.

One night after the team had struggled to beat Villanova, I curled up in our green velvet chair in front of the living room fireplace waiting for Dick to come home. When he arrived, he tossed his overcoat across the couch and slumped into the opposite chair. He unpinned his trademark green carnation from his lapel and threw it into the fire. His leisure suits and polka dot shirts of the early seventies had given way to pinstripes, vests, and double-breasted jackets.

"Winning ugly is still winning," I opened.

"Tell the local critics that. They'll be all over me because we didn't run Rollie and the boys out on a rail."

"Why the sloppy performance?"

"It was a 'must' win," Dick said. "I could tell the team was a little off, a little tired. Just one of those nights when you're going to beat yourself. Frankly, we were lucky to win."

"I'm beginning to understand why Katie Parseghian never went to the football games. This isn't much fun anymore."

"Sometimes it is. I still love working with the kids, I love the strategy, preparing for games. The other stuff isn't important." Dick got up and went into the kitchen to get a beer. In an hour he would have shrugged it all off. Not me. I pulled it all inside and let it fester. The girl who wanted to be a coach's wife was gone. Another woman had taken her place, one who knew that baking cookies wouldn't cut it. But what would?

Dick patted my head as he walked by my chair on his way to the TV room to catch the late news. "Just hang in there with me. I need you to talk to."

So much for getting off the fast track. That isn't a decision that we can make. One day we discover that the decision has been made for us, or we missed the moment when we could have chosen otherwise. In any case, there are no exits, just coping strategies.

At the same time a sea change was occurring in the kind of women who were coming to Notre Dame. Dick hired Danny Nee (now head coach at Nebraska) as an assistant coach and Danny brought his wife Chris with him. Chris taught school, gave birth to their son Patrick, and immediately returned to teaching. That raised a few eyebrows among the older women associated with the athletic department, but it was clear that I was no longer an anomaly in my insistence on a life and career of my own. Chris brought me into a circle of younger wives, all of whom worked and had families; and none of whom saw themselves as lovelywives. I was no longer burdened with the "Head Coach's Wife" label. I was becoming acccpted, slowly, for myself.

So many years later, we easily defeated Portland, a victory at last, a "must" win, but Dick and the assistant coaches, Matty, Fran, and Jeff, had little time to celebrate. They huddled at the party, worried about the incoming grade reports. LaPhonso Ellis appeared headed for trouble again. That tough first-semester junior year loomed for all accounting majors, with even strong students pulling their first D's in courses. So it was for LaPhonso, but with Notre Dame's eligiblity requirement at 2.0, he couldn't afford to many D's. Still Dick has encouraged him to stay in accounting. "How many NBA players have accounting degrees?" he asked him. "Hang tough. Don't sell yourself short."

I circulated, thinking that this might well be my last postgame party. Outside snow fell gently and Christmas lights blinked on as night approached. The ghosts of Christmases past paraded before me—the years when the players could not go home (because of the Kentucky game in neutral Louisville). Memories, cemented in faded photographs and old home movies, chronicle our years here, our children growing up among the different groups of players. The players came to our house for meals and gift exchanges, occasions which always dissolved into hilarity. We gathered the gifts into a pillowcase, and Dick, dressed as Santa, ho-ho-ho-ed into the room to distribute them. The players would rub their eyes in disbelief. Could this be the ferocious Digger? The one who roared at them in practice and at games? In that ridiculous red suit?

The gifts, limited to five dollars, were always gags, the giver capitalizing on some idiosyncrasy, or nickname, or embarrassing event, often well known to the players. John Shumate, for example, received a toy telephone because of loquacious Shu's tendency to run up sizable phone bills. Tracy Jackson once received a "Mr. Potato Head" game because Bill Hanzlik, who nicknamed all his teammates, had endowed him with that name. Someone gave Stan Wilcox a pint of cheap whisky in a brown paper bag, "for his future on park benches" the card read. (Stan is now a lawyer.) Kelly Tripuka, on the cutting edge of fashion with his newly curled hair, received a home permanent kit, complete with pink plastic rods to keep his curls in shape. Mike Mitchell once got a pair of lace pantyhose. The players found it very funny, although its significance was (happily) a mystery to us.

These memory scenes unrolled through time, the players seeming like an endless, invisible team. And this party blended with all the other parties as the snow fell slowly, covering the blue spruce along the alleyway behind our house, covering the backyard like an endless question.

Most of my guests left and I took off my shoes and fell into a chair to have a last drink with the stragglers—Tex and Brigid, Sharon and Brian, Mary and Fred, John and Mary.

"Good job, Richard!" John said. "An impressive win today." Dear John, the perfect fan.

"And Christmas!" Sharon bubbled.

Tex and Brigid were leaving just after the New Year for six months in England where Tex would direct Notre Dame's law program there. "So when are you going to direct the London program, Terry?" Tex asked. "You're perfect for it and it's time we had a female director."

London! What a thought! Thousands of miles away from

basketball. "Someday," I replied. "When Dick gets out of coaching so he can go with me."

"Now, Richard," John said, "don't do anything precipitous. These young men need you."

"Right, John," Dick laughed. "And the fans need me, too. Who else can they heap so much abuse on?"

Everyone joined in the laughter. It felt all right, in perspective, the way it should. I stood and raised my glass. "To a win," with a nod to John, "and to Christmas," with a nod to Sharon. "Merry Christmas, everyone!"

13

———

New Year 1991 arrived one late December night and we hardly noticed. The Christmas that I hoped to make so happy came and went in a blur and we rang in the new year with a mixture of joy and sadness.

One of those ominous calls came again at 5 A.M. on the day of Christmas Eve. It was Jamie and my heart stopped, fearing that Karen had lost their baby. No good news comes at 5 A.M. Jamie said that Dick's father had collapsed and was on his way to the hospital in an ambulance. Margaret and Dick Sr., Dick's parents, were staying for the holidays at Karen and Jamie's more spacious new house (with its numerous bathrooms). My father-in-law had been ill a few months earlier and had his spleen removed due to a blood disorder. He fell the evening before and in the very early morning, Karen heard him groaning. She and Jamie immediately summoned paramedics and an ambulance. Margaret rode with him to the hospital. Throughout that day and all of Christmas day, the doctors tried to avoid surgery they feared he would not survive. Finally on December 26 our friend Dr. Howard Engel told us that the surgeons had to go in and find out why his vital signs were not improving. "It's a huge risk," he said. "I'm not very optimistic, but we can't let him stay in this condition. It will surely kill him." We could trust Howard to be blunt, he was known for it. But he was also a loving and compassionate man, one who called me out of the blue from time to time just to make sure I was feeling all right. He also called after particularly tough games this year to ask me how Dick was doing. He wouldn't let me brush it off with a "Fine, we're doing great."

"Bullshit!" he'd say. "This has got to be hell for both of you." He was clearly not enjoying having to give us bad news about Dick's father. His brusqueness masked a secret softness that I had come to love. "I don't like this at all," he said to Margaret, Dick, and Dick's sisters who had flown in. "If we could wait, we would. But we can't."

Dick was nervous and short-tempered, so we made him go to practice and promised to call him as soon as the surgery was over. His much-needed Christmas break from basketball had been spent at his father's bedside. The surgery revealed internal bleeding that the doctors were able to stop, and at last everything was all right. Perhaps our luck was changing. Or perhaps we just spent it all on something other than winning a basketball game. The games—the wins, the losses, the attitude of Notre Dame—took on a new perspective.

The new year was but a week old and Dick's sisters had gone home, the family vigil no longer necessary. My father-in-law was slowly recovering enough to return home to Beacon, a journey we had feared he would never make. And Dick had left for the long January road trip that was typically scheduled while the players were on semester break. Timmy still could not play and the team faced games against North Carolina, the U.S.S.R., Wichita State, and Miami. The grade reports were in and LaPhonso would not be eligible once the second semester started, having failed to get the requisite 2.0 during the fall semester.

In the days when Dick controlled the schedule, he used this January road trip to take the players who lived far away from South Bend to play near their hometowns. That way friends and family who could not afford to travel could see them play. I went along when we could afford both a baby-sitter and my plane ticket. One year stands out in particular when I went on the trip to see Gilberto Salinas play in San Antonio, Orlando Woolridge in Shreveport, and Mike Mitchell in San Francisco. It was great to watch the pride on the family members' faces when the starting lineup was announced; I loved seeing the old high school buddies treat their now-renowned former schoolmates with atypical deference.

Dick tried to schedule activities other than basketball for the players in the various cities in which they played. In New York, for example, he usually took the players to Wall Street, once having Willie Frye, a former Notre Dame football player turned Wall Streeter, provide them with a guided tour of the stock exchange. The Notre Dame network is a vital and loyal one, and wherever the team went, they found Notre Dame alumni more than willing not only to attend the game but also to accommodate the team in other ways. The Shreveport/San Antonio trip was a perfect example of that. In Shreveport, former Notre Dame football player and air force colonel Jack Lee took us on a tour of the SAC base, allowed us inside some control headquarters, and explained the fail-safe system that SAC has in place. For some reason, the player for whom the game was scheduled always played the worst game of his career in front of the hometown fans. Orlando Woolridge, the Shreveport native, put in an uncharacteristically poor performance that night, but we won the game. And Orlando, despite his off-game, was the hero for the hometown fans.

In San Antonio, Gilberto Salinas's hometown, Mrs. Salinas picked me up early at the hotel to give me an insider's tour of the city, including the huge marketplace. She took me for genuine huevos rancheros and filled me with local lore. Like Orlando, Gilberto played one of his worst games ever, exiting, nonetheless, to loud cheers from family and friends.

After the game, the whole team was treated to a horseback ride and dinner at a dude ranch in nearby Bandera, compliments of Notre Dame graduate Don Hicks and his wife, Judy. Tracy Jackson, from Washington, D.C. (where one rarely sees a cowboy), perched precariously atop his horse, not sure that he liked this roughing it much at all. "So, Tracy, you going to move down here after graduation?" someone yelled. Tracy just looked a little grimmer and held on more tightly to the saddle horn. "I hope I live through this so I *can* graduate!"

Tracy survived and we moved on to San Francisco, Mike Mitchell's hometown, to play the University of San Francisco. Rick Masucci, a big fan, was the hotel manager and he saw to it that we had the best suite in the hotel—complete with butler and complimentary hors d'oeuvres. When Jim Roemer, who was in San Francisco visiting his sons, showed up, we pretended that this was how we always stayed on the road. The butler, Russell, grabbed the gift of sourdough bread and wine from Tim Roemer, Jim's son, and brought it back sliced and poured, on silver and in crystal. Dick and I tried to keep straight faces, complicitous in the charade that this sort of thing happened all the time. As soon as Russell left the room, though, we burst out laughing.

"Damn!" Jim said. "You Phelpses sure know how to live!"

"I'm a little embarrassed," Tim, then a college student (now a member of Congress representing our district), said. "That's pretty cheap wine. It really belongs in paper cups, not Waterford crystal."

"Well, I hope you two will try and behave yourselves and not embarrass us in front of Russell," I chided them. "He thinks we're pretty high class—or at least he *did* until you two arrived."

Even with Jim and his sons cheering us on, along with Father Bill Toohey who was spending a sabbatical year at Berkeley, we lost to San Francisco, one of the last years before its basketball program was suspended because of numerous scandals and NCAA violations. But the trip was an unmitigated success. Everyone was happy; we felt like a family.

That trip filled with friends, family, and activities was fun, although traveling with the team was not necessarily a good time. On the one hand, it was restful not to have to make any decisions about much of anything for a while. You were told where to show up, when the bus was leaving, where and what you were eating. It had a certain mindless relaxation about it. This was particularly true of the trips abroad that we'd been able to take every four years. Many foreign countries were anxious to have American college teams visit and play exhibition games against their national team. That way the national team could hone its skills against some good competition before competing in the various world competitions. The NCAA allowed college teams to go abroad once every four years. Our first trip in 1975 was a memorable exception to the mindless relaxation norm. It began calmly enough. We traveled first to Italy and holed up for a week in a hotel on the outskirts of Milan. The players became bored and unhappy rather quickly. They couldn't get their usual brand of cereal for breakfast; the television shows were all in *Italian!* The hotel was somewhat isolated and the players had little to do during the day except wonder when they were going to be able to get home. The only high point was the Italians' response to Bill Paterno. Golden boy Billy, with his blond hair, blue eyes, and Italian surname, was a crowd favorite. "Cinquant-cinque" (fifty-five, Bill's uniform number) they would chant when Billy handled the ball. "Cinquant-cinque, cinquant-cinque" filled the arena.

The players were not taking well to world travel when, at the end of the week, we went to the Milan airport to catch a plane to Madrid where we would play games against Real Madrid for a few days and finish out the tour. After our indifferent Italian hosts left us at the airport doors, we discovered that we had to pay substantial additional lira to be allowed to take the trunks filled with the uniforms and trainer's supplies with us. Then we discovered that our plane to Madrid was canceled. When we finally caught another flight over six hours later, we had not been able to contact our hosts in Madrid to tell them that we would be arriving late. We landed at the Madrid airport with no one to greet us and no clue as to where we were staying. My husband, his assistant Dick Kuchen, and I sat balanced on trunks and suitcases trying to figure out what to do and trying to calm the tired and annoyed players: Paterno, Toby Knight, Dave Batton, and the rest of the team were becoming increasingly sorry that they had ever left the United States. Dick Kuchen and I, self-impressed with our high school Spanish, tried calling all the large hotels to see if any had reservations for an American team. "Me llama es Ricardo Kuchen," Kuch began.

"Yes, sir. Can I help you?" a voice replied in English, obviously not taken in by Kuch's fluency. Kuch got to practice his Spanish, but we discovered nothing about our destination. We tried calling the American embassy but since it was now after midnight, we got no answer. Just when we were faced with mutiny from the team, who had collectively decided that finding a flight back to the States was in order (never mind that we had no way of paying for it), someone showed up to collect us and delivered our weary bodies to our hotel.

Those were the unusual trips. I was usually on my own on the typical road trip. Dick was not much fun, obsessed with game tapes and team meetings. Although he was always relaxed enough after games, win or lose, *before* games he was unapproachable. He had his game-face on and I stayed out of his way. He was in his own little world; he would dress deliberately, focused inward. For him, the pregame tension escalated and reached its peak in the half hour before the game began. "The pressure closes in on you," he said. He would put music on in the locker room or kid around with Ed O'Rourke, a loyal fan who traveled to most of the away games and had a regular seat behind the bench, but nothing alleviated the pressure, which had intensified in recent years. When we had gone to see the movie *Hoosiers*, Dick had resonated with one particular scene: the coach, played by Gene Hackman, goes into a barbershop in the small town in which he coaches high school basketball. The men in the shop tell him what they expect of him: the style of play they want, the results he better deliver. "That's what pregame feels like," Dick said. "Faceless fans saying, 'you'd better deliver, and it better be our way.' Pregame tension will finally drive me out of coaching."

I stayed at home this year, unable to go on the road trip, and tried not to be stressed out. It was bitterly cold, the ground constantly snow-covered, the sun rarely shining, the weather service delivering frequent blizzard warnings, a common South Bend phenomenon that was all too frequently followed by the real thing. In fact, in the late seventies a blizzard shut down the whole town for nearly a week. Well, almost the whole town—a basketball game managed to go on.

Snow began to fall just before a basketball game with West Virginia. After a couple of days and nights, when it finally stopped, the snow was window-ledge high. The airport, schools, stores all were closed; Notre Dame even canceled classes. The unfortunate West Virginia basketball team not only lost the game but also sat trapped in a local motel. Neighbors pooled resources and impromptu dinner parties sprang up in the neighborhoods. Children, freed from school for the duration, celebrated with snowball fights and rolled around in the tremendous drifts. We slowly dug out with our neighbors and one of the neighborhood teenagers walked to the nearest store to stock up on milk and bread for everyone.

A game with the University of Maryland was scheduled for Sunday, but it looked like it would surely be postponed: the police had forbidden motorists to drive and the airport remained closed. Dick managed to get to practice by hitching rides on snow plows and the players waded through the snow from their dorm rooms. But the game must go on. A single plane was finally allowed into the airport on Saturday and it carried the Maryland basketball team and the NBC crew to televise the game. On its way out, it carried the West Virginia players, now suffering from near-terminal cabin fever and ecstatic to be returning to "Almost Heaven." Since no one was allowed to drive, Notre Dame officials announced via local television and radio that they would admit anyone willing to walk to the game, ticket or not.

On Sunday afternoon two hours before the game, the roads to the basketball arena looked like the roads approaching a famous shrine. Thousands of the faithful walked, as pilgrims to Canterbury, in the direction of the great white domes of the Athletic and Convocation Center. Karen, then thirteen, had broken her leg skiing a few weeks earlier, so the McFadden boys bundled her onto a toboggan and Dennis McFadden pulled her the mile to the campus. The students, not relegated by their student tickets to a single section of the arena as usual, sat in the stands surrounding the court. It was one of the liveliest and loudest games ever, not only because of the novel seating arrangement but also because it was the first chance to get out in several days for many of the students and townspeople. Notre Dame upset a ranked Maryland team, snow plows began to clear the South Bend streets, and life returned to normal.

Normal? A month later we were on our way to Tulsa, Oklahoma, for the first round of the NCAA tournament. The University paid for the wives to go to tournament games so Chris Nee, Georgia Kuchen, Susan McLaughlin, and I decided to pass the time by having a tournament of our own: tennis. When the Tulsa Alumni Club called and asked if they could do anything for us, we had one request—a tennis court.

A week later we traveled to Lawrence, Kansas, for the regionals. While national attention was focused on which team would emerge to go to the Final Four, Chris, Susan, Georgia, and

I battled it out on a tennis court on the University of Kansas campus. I was still winning and a green T-shirt that Chris designed for first prize hung in the balance. The basketball team also won and all of us returned home to pack up for St. Louis for the Final Four—and the finals of the Notre Dame Basketball Coaches' Wives Traveling Tennis Match.

Another blizzard hit just after the team landed in St. Louis and hundreds of Notre Dame fans were forced to spend the night in shelters along Interstate 55. The tennis tournament was driven indoors, and we, with our minimal tennis skills but boundless enthusiasm, were entertained at a posh St. Louis tennis club, greeted by a pro in silks to warm up with us. We had become so obsessed with playing tennis at every tournament site that people began to think we were serious tennis players. Not at all. We were just superstitious. If *we* kept playing so would the team. The skills of Laimbeer, Flowers, Jackson and Tripucka doubtless contributed to the victories, but we were convinced of the magic link between our tennis and the team's success.

Dick's enthusiasm was also boundless, boyish, unsophisticated. Since our days in our little apartment in Hazleton, Pennsylvania, he had wondered what it would be like to be at the Final Four. Through the years, he had promised innumerable people that they would be part of it if he ever made it to the Final Four. After we beat DePaul in the regionals, he spent hours handing out tickets, delivering on his promise.

When Notre Dame took the floor of the arena in St. Louis, he felt like a kid at Christmas: "I'm finally here!" Unfortunately Laimbeer and Flowers could not shut down Duke's Gminski and Duke went ahead by 16 in the first half of the semifinal game. Late in the game, we pulled within 2 points, with the ball. But Duck Williams missed the tying basket and Duke won by 4.

Dick's spirits remained high. He left our room early Easter morning to search around St. Louis for stuffed bunnies to distribute to the athletic department children who would be with their parents at the morning Mass. All this was in stark contrast to the grim, determined faces on the Kentucky fans, all of whom who were wearing "I love Joe B." buttons in honor of the coach they had nearly driven out of Lexington two years earlier. "Déjà vu all over again," I mused, wondering once again what it was about winning basketball games that led people to abandon their senses.

Luckily for Joe B. Hall, Kentucky won the national championship that year. And we lost the consolation game to Arkansas (in one of the last years the NCAA forced teams to play it) when Montcrieff hit a nearly half-court buzzer shot over Bill Hanzlik. After the Final Four, what we naively had seen as a shining moment for Notre Dame basketball, we returned to South Bend to criticism: "Christ, they only came in fourth!" "I heard Digger let everybody have fun out there! He doesn't take this seriously enough!"

One year later we spent St. Patrick's Day in Indianapolis waiting to play the following day in the regional finals against Michigan State led by Magic Johnson. Wisdom had it that the winner of that game would win the national championship. Bill Hanzlik, who had developed into a superb defensive player, held Magic to a reasonable performance, but Greg Kelser, Michigan State's "other" player, played brilliantly and we lost by 11. We went home; Michigan State went on to play against Indiana State and Larry Bird and won the national championship that year.

That was as close as we got. Although Dick's teams regularly won twenty games a year and sometimes made it to the regionals, consistency does not win fan support. Fans want the big flash, the rush that being number one brings them. It's understandable, of course, and probably wouldn't matter as long as fans never got the notion that they could control a coach's destiny. A supportive administration keeps fans' unreasonable demands in check. It also allows a coach to do his job with some integrity.

But the atmosphere in Notre Dame sports was beginning to remind me of a sixteenth-century Italian court: intrigues, whispers—Who's in? Who's out? Who's got the power? Who's out to get whom? Who's filling the coffers? Talking behind backs, veiled glances, double-edged remarks, an occasional public attack. Notre Dame seemed gripped in a Mafia-style "omerta," a vow of silence. However ugly things may be below the surface, one did not speak of them. Even the truth was frowned upon.

Frowned upon? No, shunned and ridiculed as the Cordellis found out. Pete, an assistant football coach, was questioned by the NCAA about Lou Holtz's tenure as head coach at the University of Minnesota. Minnesota's athletic program was under investigation and because Pete had also been an assistant there, as well as with Holtz at North Carolina State and Arkansas, he was questioned about certain activities. Pete had come into Dick's office shaking. "What the hell should I do?" he asked Dick. "Should I lie?"

"Just tell the truth, Pete," Dick had said. "If you tell the truth, everything will be all right. You know that."

Wrong. Because Pete's story differed from Holtz's, Pete and Laurie were shunned, ostracized, and publicly ridiculed. At a Christmas party, an assistant athletic director lambasted Pete while Laurie stood in the room, trying to disappear into the woodwork. She fought back tears of rage and kept her mouth shut like a proper lovelywife.

So do I as I get more and more used to being shunned by assistant athletic directors who had been our friends. At a party shortly before Christmas, I walked over to talk to someone and he cut me off cold. I turned to Jenny, who was with me. "Am I getting paranoid? Or did he just look through me and walk away?"

"You're right, Mom. He pretended he didn't see you."

Luckily for Laurie and Pete, Pete found a head coaching job and was leaving Notre Dame. He had committed the ultimate sin; there was no way he could stay.

It was tempting to avoid, as much as was possible, anything that was Notre Dame. Instead, though, I tried to stay focused on the Notre Dame that transcended all the meanness. One blizzardy Saturday when the team was playing on the road and I had been shut in for over twenty-four hours, I called my friend Sonia Gernes, a novelist, poet, and professor in the English department. "Let's go cross-country skiing, Sonia. I'll walk over to your house and we can ski from there on the path that runs along the river." As I skied in the narrow wake of Sonia's skis and listened to her talk of the problems she was encountering while revising her new novel, the sun came out and my world gathered light.

14

In my Law and Literature seminar, we began the new term by discussing why law students should bother reading works of literature. They're going to be lawyers, aren't they? Why read novels?

My teaching career at Notre Dame began when I was assigned to teach Freshman Composition and Literature as part of my graduate work. I hadn't actually thought about being a teacher; I continued with school because I enjoyed it so much. But with the teaching, I found something that I loved as much as Dick loved coaching. I was terrified the first few times I met my freshman class on the fourth floor of the administration building. My "pre-class tension" would mount as I climbed the flights of stairs to the classroom under the Golden Dome. But once inside the room, once the class began, I became absorbed in the students' eagerness to learn. I countered their questions with more questions, I pushed their imaginations: "What does Ibsen *mean* by that door slam at the end of *A Doll's House?* Where is Nora going? What do you think J. Alfred Prufrock looks like?" Some students drew pictures for me. My fears of disappearing into the lovelywife receded forever as I introduced Notre Dame freshmen to the wonders of T. S. Eliot's "The Love Song of J. Alfred Prufrock," the horrors of Elie Wiesel's *Night,* and the effectiveness of paragraph transitions and the active voice. I was good at this! They listened, they learned, and I thrived. In addition to teaching, I took courses, studied for comprehensive examinations, and began a dissertation.

Began. A few years later, I discovered that to begin does not necessarily mean to finish. So I stopped all extra activities and set myself to the task of finally becoming a Ph.D. (instead of a lifelong ABD—All But Dissertation). To underscore this conviction, I made a habit of telling everyone I ran into that I would be graduating that year—so that I would be too embarrassed to slack off on my work.

During my "How are you/I'm graduating this year" phase, I met the dean of the law school, Dave Link. Dave asked me what plans I had beyond graduation. "To be quite frank," I said, "I can hardly think beyond the next chapter of my dissertation. Since I have so little geographic flexibility, I'll just have to see what turns up." That was my official stance; in truth I hoped desperately to avoid the exploitation that happened to so many well-educated wives in isolated college towns. Advanced degrees in hand, eager to teach, unable to move because of a husband's job, they were forced to take adjunct positions that paid nearly nothing. The amount of money didn't concern me personally, but the exploitation aroused my feminist ire. I wanted to teach when I received my Ph.D. But at what price?

"I have a job for which you might interview," Dave said. "It's only part time, but with your experience in teaching composition, you might be interested. We are trying to do something about our legal writing program. Traditionally it's taught by lawyers, but that doesn't seem to work very well. We're thinking of trying an experienced writing teacher."

What a radical idea, I thought cynically. Out loud I said, "Let me think about it. I'll give you a call."

Teaching in a law school was not what I had planned to do, but as I turned the idea over in my mind, I found it more and more intriguing. I had toyed with going to law school after I had completed my undergraduate work, but the lure of all those wonderful books to read in a literature program won out. Nonetheless, the law fascinated me and the law school seemed far less ivory tower than the English department. Lawyers had real power; I would be teaching people who just might change the world. As I looked beyond my graduate work, I found the prospect of teaching in a law school interesting. I called the dean and set up an appointment for an interview.

The details of that interview have become apocryphal. The dean claims I said he was crazy when he told me that the *part-time* job he had in mind involved teaching 160 first-year law students. In his version of the interview, he says that he offered me the job because I told him that he didn't know what he was talking about. He says he knew that he didn't know what he was talking about, and he wanted someone, like me, who knew more than he did about teaching writing. The truth, as I remember it, is that I *thought* he was crazy but that I was far too diplomatic to say it. I said that it would have to be a full-time job if he wanted it done well, that one does not teach writing by injection, but with workshops, numerous assignments, revisions, and plenty of teacher intervention. "Labor intensive" is what we call it in the business.

"Labor intensive" was a considerable understatement. I finished my dissertation, received my Ph.D. in August, and began teaching in the law school two weeks later. It took all my resources just to keep my head above water—so much of it was entirely new to me. I took the job because I thought it would be challenging and because I figured that if I did well I might have a future in the position, as I probably would not if I took a visiting position in the English department which was unlikely to hire permanently one of its own graduates. The law school job was worth giving a try.

Eleven years later I'm a full professor on the law school faculty. To the dean's credit, I have been given all the space I need to succeed or fail. I came in fresh, knowing nothing about traditional law school pedagogy so I invented my own. I now have ten teaching assistants whom I train to conduct weekly workshops, and the first-year law students write, and rewrite, office memoranda, client letters, and briefs with plenty of teacher and peer input during the writing process. The law school regularly receives accolades from judges and law firms about the noticeably superior writing skills of our graduates. It's an exhausting and consuming job and I love it. I particularly love the individual work I'm able to do with students who might not have the writing skills to get through law school exams. Since I see so much of the students' writing early in their first semester, I'm able to recognize who might have problems and get involved before failure occurs.

And my work has brought Dick and me closer. My tutorial work with my own students has made me more sensitive to the academic struggles that some of his players endure. Dick finds my colleagues and law school events a welcome diversion from the pressures of coaching. He is tickled to be introduced as "Richard, Professor Phelps' spouse." He is even pleased when the occasional academic asks him, "And what do you do for a living, Mr. Phelps?"

A few years ago, during the February heat of basketball season, Dick joined me at a law school dinner for the Moot Court team. We were seated at a table with Tex and Brigid Dutile, my friend and colleague Patty O'Hara, and a visiting professor (Professor X) who had never met Dick. Professor X was a pompous little man, often silly and self-absorbed. But he was also endearing at times and the faculty had grown accustomed to his peculiar ways. Dick rushed into the University Club, his hair still damp from his postpractice shower. We were playing Marquette the next day, an intense rivalry, and Dick looked forward to a few hours of non-basketball talk to relieve the pressure he was feeling. He searched out the empty seat beside me, slid into it, and ordered a beer. My friends had barely uttered greetings when Professor X started in: "Oh, are you like Bobby Knight? Do you throw chairs, too?"

Dick shot me a puzzled look. "Oh, I'd better be careful," Professor X persisted, "he looks like he's going to throw that chair." Tex, Brigid, and Patty started to giggle.

"No," Dick said patiently, "I don't throw chairs."

"Nice weather we're having." Brigid tried to change the subject. I was desperately avoiding Patty's eye and biting my lip to suppress my own giggles.

"Well, I never go to games," Professor X continued. "I won't be there tomorrow to see you in your fancy suit and green carnation." Dick looked quickly at me and Patty. "This is a setup, right?" he said under his breath.

"No," said Professor X, "I'll be where I am every Saturday— at the Grotto praying. I'll be there praying while you're at that basketball game." Patty and I were now gasping for breath and tears streamed down our faces, evidence of our not-so-silent laughter. People at nearby tables began to notice and tuned in to the conversation.

Tex turned to Brigid. "The dinner is going well, don't you think, dear?"

"Are you like Woody Hayes, then? Do you hit people?" Professor X was relentless.

"Terry," Dick finally said, "if you want a divorce, just ask for one. Don't put me through this."

"I don't like sports myself," Professor X went on. "So I don't bother going to games. But I'll pray for you at the Grotto tomorrow." Patty and I had completely lost control. Students and faculty at other tables began to titter.

"Yes," said Brigid to Tex, "a wonderful party. Our friends are getting along so well."

"No, thanks," Dick said to Professor X. "Remember what

happened to the last guy who prayed at the Grotto," an oblique reference to Gerry Faust.

"Who is it you're playing tomorrow? Do you have a chance against them?" Professor X renewed the inquisition. I finally took pity on Dick and mustered up my self-control. "Come on, honey," I said to Dick as I stood up, "I'd like you to meet the guest judges." I drew him away from the table, leaving Patty, Tex, and Brigid dissolving in their seats and Professor X oblivious to the show he had put on.

"Stories," I told the students enrolled in Law and Literature, a new course I developed a few years ago, "make you better lawyers, not because they show you your moral duty, but because they show you how your membership in the legal profession relates to your general aim to live well, to live integrated, good lives. Stories demonstrate that rules divorced from the narratives in which they are embedded make bad law and bad lawyers. Abstracted law lures us away from the messy world in which we live and seduces us into believing that we (as lawyers) have things under control."

To prove this we read and discussed *Antigone, Billy Budd, Huckleberry Finn,* Martin Luther King's "Letter from Birmingham Jail," and many other works that throw the civil law into conflict with moral law. As third-year students soon to be lawyers, the students needed to know that the law could not be our god.

What are our gods? My students delineated money and success in addition to the law. "Sports," one suggested. "Especially here. I experienced nothing like it at my undergraduate school."

"Yes, sports," I said and let it drop, not wanting to intertwine my two lives, especially not then, when the worship of money and winning had made me touchy and cynical.

We had four home games to play in the next two weeks—against West Virginia, Marquette, Rutgers, and Virginia. After beating West Virginia fairly easily on Tuesday night, on Wednesday after practice Dick and I attended a dinner/spiritual reflection group of which we'd been a part for a year or so. This was a group of people from Notre Dame who were trying to integrate their spiritual and professional lives, who wanted to find some space in their busy schedules for reflection, for prayer, and for meeting with others with the same concerns. I had always been drawn to groups such as this, and many times I attended alone. That year I asked Dick to come along, detecting that he too felt that a sense of spiritual mission was slipping out of his life. The group gathered for dinner every few weeks and each person provided a dish. After dinner, we had some time for reflection, discussion, and prayer. The group had come to mean a great deal to us, gave us something of a center that held, and reminded us why we remained at Notre Dame. That night as we stood around talking before dinner, someone came in and announced, "I just heard it on the car radio—we are bombing Kuwait!"

Somehow I have never rid myself of the sound of bombs, although I have no conscious memories of the bombing of London. Nonetheless, since grade school films about war, I have found myself shaking and crying whenever I hear certain sounds. As our friends turned to watch the television and CNN's on-the-spot coverage of our warplanes and rockets hitting Kuwait, I quietly retreated to a hallway and wept silently. I had prayed so hard that this would not happen, would not be necessary, and it took some time for me to regain my composure enough to rejoin the group. Dick found me and put his arms around me, as my childhood terror slowly dissipated.

Some schools had canceled games because of the war and there was some talk at Notre Dame about at least postponing the Marquette game. We went ahead and played, but Dick requested a moment of silence before the game—for all the victims of war. When he and I discussed his doing so, I particularly asked that he avoid nationalistic fervor and pray for all the victims. This war, I feared, would have few winners.

During the game some students ran around the stands with a long banner, cheering on our troops. The crowd erupted with approval, but I felt chilled to the bone. It's far too easy to mix up sports and war—the vocabulary is even the same: words like "battle," "fight," "victors." These college students, too young to remember Vietnam, see United States versus Iraq as just another game, just as their intensity over who wins games confuses a game with war.

We beat Marquette, adjusting to LaPhonso's absence, then lost to Rutgers, and came quite close to upsetting a highly ranked Virginia team. We went ahead by a single point with a few seconds to go and Virginia turned the ball over. We had the ball under Virginia's basket and our player could not get it inbounds. He opted for a long pass downcourt—to no one—and the ball went out of bounds. Because no one touched it, Virginia got the ball back under their own basket and scored in the final second to win the game. Dick ate the player's mistake, as he should, saying at the postgame press conference that the long pass was a viable option and that if a player had been downcourt as assigned, it would have worked perfectly.

After the game, Karen went with Jamie and a few friends to Rocco's, the local legendary Italian restaurant. As she sat eating pizza in a booth, she overheard a woman loudly denouncing the game, its outcome, and particularly the coach. "I can't stand watching that stupid coach anymore," the woman proclaimed to everyone within earshot, drawing doubtless on years of coaching experience.

Karen, not one to duck confrontation, stopped at the woman's table on her way out of the restaurant. "I'm Karen Phelps," she said, "and that's my father you were talking about." The woman turned white. "Perhaps you should think before you open your mouth," Karen continued and turned dramatically on her heel.

In the next week, we had to play four more games—that's four games in eight days—against Dayton (on the road), Boston College, Duke, and LaSalle. It was beginning to feel like a professional basketball schedule. Dick was hoping to win two of the four, knowing that fatigue was going to catch up with them. The players—the "student-athletes"—struggled to attend class and keep up with all their schoolwork.

I struggled too—to persevere patiently, to be supportive, to keep my mouth shut, to know my place, to keep smiling at *all* the games—to be the perfect lovelywife.

15

We did win two of the four games exactly as Dick said he expected. But he was far from happy. Truth was, he wanted, some part of him even expected, to win all four, despite the odds against it. He was the eternal optimist—the cutting down of the nets in practice before the 1974 UCLA game was a fitting symbol of the fact that he always was convinced that his team could beat *anybody*. Although he tried to sound realistic, tried to remember that he was patching together a team without three starters, he could not quench his nature and was profoundly disappointed. "We should have been able to beat Duke at home," he insisted. "After the way we played them in the NIT—we had a shot at them."

"You had LaPhonso for the NIT," I pointed out.

And he was spending nearly every waking hour preparing for each game following so quickly on another game's heels. After an impressive 16-point victory over LaSalle, he arrived home after midnight. No drinks at the club for him these days; no chance however briefly to celebrate. Just game tapes and more game tapes. In three days, we would play Syracuse. I had been worried about the players getting tired. As I watched Dick take off his shirt, once drenched from the game but dry hours later, I noticed how exhausted he seemed, older, moving more slowly and deliberately. The year had aged him.

"Friday is Fred's birthday. Mary wants to know if we can go to their house for dinner. Do you think you can get away for a few hours?" I asked.

"Terry, I don't know. We play Syracuse Saturday," he replied impatiently. "Besides, I'm not much in the mood for a party."

I began to get a little testy. This long-suffering wife routine was wearing thin. "I *know* you play Syracuse Saturday. It's not a party—just the four of us. I have to tell Mary something. Shall I say we can't make it?"

"No. I'll go after practice Friday. But it can't be a late night."

"Right." I turned out the light. No point in asking him to pick up something for Fred's birthday.

By Friday all hell had broken loose. A newspaper in Syracuse had run stories implicating some Syracuse players in serious infractions. Syracuse turned itself in to the NCAA, temporarily suspended seven players, and awaited NCAA action. It looked as though Syracuse would show up in South Bend, for a game to be nationally televised by CBS, with walk-ons ready to take the court.

Dick and I had hardly spoken for days, less by design (although it wasn't a bad idea) than because Dick was totally absorbed in preparing for the game. He left the house before I got up and returned after I had gone to bed. There was really no point in trying to talk to him. Thank God I would get to spend some time with Fred and Mary, who always made me laugh, with whom I didn't have to maintain appearances. They had both been around sports enough so that they knew about "game-faces." I wouldn't have to apologize, as I felt I did too much of the time, if Dick was less than charming. They understood that before and during a game, Dick was working, although what he did looked like recreation, in fact *was* recreation for everyone else.

I went to the Ferlics' alone earlier than Dick since we couldn't be sure what time he could show up. The same was always true for Fred, who was frequently delayed in surgery. Neither had put in an appearance before I arrived. I sat with Mary in the kitchen as she prepared dinner. "You're taking this cooking stuff pretty seriously, aren't you?" I was teasing her—I love to cook and Mary has always hated it. But lately Mary seemed to have settled on some kind of truce with the kitchen.

"You make it look so easy. I figured if you could do it I could." She was teasing me back, which was one of the best things about our friendship. We're very different and we seemed to absorb things from each other. Mary helped me be better at things I don't take to naturally—community fund-raising, for example— and I did likewise with her. And Mary, blessed with a capacity for friendship, had brought new people into our life.

"God, Mary, will this basketball season ever be over? Dick is so uptight, he's getting impossible to live with. I just try and stay out of his way."

Mary just shrugged. As a doctor's wife, she's used to handling things on her own. Doctors can be as absorbed in their work as coaches, and the hours are often as demanding.

"At least Fred doesn't have to operate in the arena. With thousands of fans second-guessing every decision he makes."

"Nor do reporters create entire columns out of his 'mistakes.' "

"What mistakes?" Fred arrived and entered the kitchen just in time to defend himself.

"Sorry, Fred. Just speaking hypothetically. We know you're the perfect doctor." I stood and kissed him.

"And Mary is the perfect cook." Fred peered curiously into the pan over which Mary was fussing. "Can you leave this alone long enough to have a drink with us, Maria?"

We were halfway through our drinks when Dick arrived. We heard his voice in the hallway joking with Beth and Katie, the Ferlic girls, before we saw him. "How's he doing?" Fred asked me.

"Just terrific. We haven't spoken in days. You probably see more of him at practice than I do at home."

Dick bounced into the room. He was trying to be jovial, I could tell. I suspected it wouldn't last.

"Do you believe this Syracuse crap?" he began without introduction. "I guarantee you that we will be playing the starting team tomorrow. There's no way the NCAA is going to suspend those players and leave CBS with a nationally televised game of Notre Dame against Syracuse walk-ons. No way. What a joke all this is. Once there's so much money involved, no one can make decisions with any integrity."

"That's a little cynical." Fred handed Dick a beer. "You want to play the walk-ons?"

"You know I don't. I always want to play the best team possible. I'm just so sick of the NCAA never doing anything. When they gave SMU the death penalty two years ago, I thought there was some hope for college basketball. But that was it. Now all they do is deliver slaps on the hand. College sports are becoming a goddamned social problem, nothing to do with education anymore."

Dick was the person who had opened the can of worms a decade earlier. Recruiting violations were rampant; those of us in the business had heard story after story of huge payoffs to players and their families as inducements to attend certain schools: money, cars, clothes, jobs for parents, girls—name it—nothing was too shameful to offer or accept. In fact, a friend of ours, a reporter, had spent several months investigating a particular major basketball power and had a story about recruiting violations ready to go to press. When two of his sources said they would not be willing to testify should the magazine be sued, however, the lawyers advised against publication. Everyone *knew* what was going on—but who was willing to say that the emperor was wearing no clothes?

My husband, I'm afraid. In 1982, Dick was attending the NCAA Final Four in New Orleans. It was the second and last time that one of Dick's teams did not have a winning season and did not receive a postseason bid. In the lobby of his hotel, he engaged in what he thought was a casual conversation with Gordon White, an old friend from the Fordham year and a sportswriter for the *New York Times*. Dick said what everyone knew, including White: high school players were regularly receiving up to $10,000 to play basketball at some schools. It must have been a slow news day, for next morning's *New York Times* front page (not the sports page) carried the story with the headline: "College Coach Says Athletes Are Paid." The *New York Post*'s back page jumped on the bandwagon with a banner reading, "Name Names, Digger."

I was at home in South Bend. Dick had not told me about his conversation with White because, frankly, neither of us saw this as news—just the same old story that no one wanted to believe. When the telephone rang at 7 A.M. with a reporter wanting to talk to Dick, I wondered what was going on. When it rang incessantly before I had a chance to have a cup of coffee, I called Dick in New Orleans. "What the hell is going on? Every reporter in the country has called. And I'm not even awake yet."

"I have no idea. Let me grab some papers and find out."

He called back ten minutes later. "You're not going to believe this. Gordie White has run a story because of a conversation we had yesterday. I'm quoted as spilling the beans about recruiting violations."

Once the emperor is revealed as naked—or perhaps naked—the kingdom must spring into action. It may do one of two things: claim he is in fact clothed or find him something to wear. The first was more common. Dick, not the recruiting violators, became the target. He was accused of sour grapes, of being disgruntled, of detracting from the Final Four with his allegations. He was denounced for refusing to name the schools and players. He, for good or ill and for once and for all, established himself as the person willing to speak out about the ugliness in college sports. "Self-righteous," some called it. "Noble," said others. And you can be sure that Notre Dame's basketball program was subject to careful scrutiny from then on. Thank God we had checked out those gag gift exchanges. Denials abounded. "Digger had a bad year," one coach said. "He's making excuses."

It took a few years before denials were rendered fruitless. Dick's statement was one of those things that once said opens the floodgates. Players came forward with stories; investigations revealed how widespread the payoffs were not an anomaly but a common practice. Finally in 1984, Walter Byers, then-head of the NCAA, said, "Not only was Digger Phelps right, he underestimated the amount of money involved."

So schools cleaned up their acts, right? Wrong. Payoff procedures became more sophisticated and illegal incentives mushroomed rather than declined or disappeared. And once some rules are broken, are seen as disposable, other things, like academic integrity, likewise suffer. The NCAA tried to regulate academics by creating Proposition 48 that required that incoming athletes have a 2.0 grade point average in eleven core courses in high school and a minimum of 700 on the SATs. The purpose of the controversial Proposition 48 was to prevent schools from taking players who were not qualified for college—to curtail the exploitation of athletic ability over academic skill. An athlete with lower credentials could still receive a scholarship to a school but not play or practice the first year. He would then have only three rather than four years of eligibility. The exception was a good idea; it was designed to benefit academic late-starters and gave them a freshman year to get up to speed. Schools immediately abused the exception and accepted players as students who had no real chance of graduating once they used up their eligibility. The

NCAA thus changed the rule to say that the athlete could not receive an athletic scholarship the first year. So programs began to fill up with Prop 48 players, as they are called, who mysteriously have plenty of money to cover first-year expenses on their own. In addition schools began more and more to resort to the "JC fix." Outstanding players who did not make the Proposition 48 requirements sometimes ended up in junior colleges (JCs). There they honed their skills for two years and then moved immediately into starting positions on regular university teams—as long as they achieved a minimum academic standard at the junior college. This was the perfect fix for a limping program. No need to wait until a freshman matures; the JC fix turns a program around in a single year.

Perhaps all this wouldn't be so bad if its purpose were to give academic late-bloomers a chance. But it's not. It has one purpose and one purpose only—win games and thereby make money for the school. Colleges and universities are full of athletes who can't compete academically, who would be far better off at a different school or perhaps even playing professional basketball without going to college. Nearly every day now sports pages carry stories about schools violating NCAA rules, about cheating scandals, about arrests of athletes for rape or assault. Sports *is* a social problem.

But that night I was not in the mood to agree with Dick. I greatly respected what he did in 1982, I knew what it had cost him, and I shared his disappointment in the increased rather than decreased problems with college sports. But I was in a bad mood, one I attributed, fairly or not, directly to his semi-permanent "game-face" during the last few weeks. "So? It's partly your fault. You were right there in the beginning when television began to get so involved with college basketball."

"How so?" Mary asked.

"Tell her," I challenged him.

"In the early seventies, Eddie Einhorn had this great idea to start to televise college basketball games. He had been televising East Coast games and wanted to expand his market. He liked our program with its national rivalries, we didn't have just regional appeal, and he put us on nearly every Saturday, on UHF stations."

"I remember that," Fred interjected. "I was interning and we could watch ND play all the time. What great games—UCLA, North Carolina, Villanova—you played everybody. Hot Rod Hudley did the games—with Dick Enberg. I'll never forget Hot Rod's jumpsuits. Or Digger's leisure suits, polka dot shirts, and long sideburns."

"Einhorn sold the package to NBC in a couple of years. It was TVS-NBC for a while and Einhorn moved on to do World Wrestling—he had an unerring eye for what was about to get hot. When NBC took over college basketball, Al McGuire and Billy Packer started to do the games with Enberg. And then the money began to escalate. It's out of control now—too much money is corrupting the system. Coaches have to win so they get on TV and get all the regular-season TV revenue. And they have to get a bid to the NCAA and get a share of the millions that the NCAA makes from the tournament. A winning basketball program can put a small school on the map and keep it out of the red."

"So what's wrong with that?" Once my sparring gloves were on, I was relentless.

"Nothing if it happens naturally as a result of the players you happen to have or those you recruit legitimately who belong at your school. But that's not the way it works. Winning and making money become the ends themselves, and the players get exploited in the process. It costs too much to let kids get an education. They might get distracted by it and not win enough games. It's down to: get the bodies in there, win games, and then get rid of them. Many winning teams are full of JCs and transfers and Prop 48 players. You know the graduation statistics. No degrees, no futures—back on the streets, some of them on drugs, hanging around the playgrounds where they once were teenaged superstars."

"Not everywhere." Mary dared to jump in. "Look at your program. Everyone graduates. They're great kids."

"Yeah. And look what's happening to me. Getting driven out because we're not selling enough tickets. Graduating everybody, winning over twenty games a year, going to a tournament every year—not good enough any more." Although we had not confided the details of the Notre Dame situation to Mary and Fred, they were close enough to us to know that something was going on.

"But *you* did it!" I pressed on. "You created this monster! You wanted a big-time program here. *You* created these expectations."

"Dinner's ready," Mary said hopefully and we called a temporary truce to move into the dining room. But Dick was seething and we were not far into Mary's delicious appetizer when he picked up the argument.

"The NCAA is hopeless. *Nothing* will happen to those Syracuse players. I guarantee it. Look at the Minnesota situation— 'minor' infractions; 'unintentional' payoffs. What has happened to the truth? Even around here?"

"Dick, give it up. That's not your problem. It's not your program. The NCAA is not your personal burden. You're obsessing over things that you can't control, can't fix. It's making you crazy. And you sound so self-righteous."

"Or is it noble?" Mary asked.

By dessert the conversation between me and Dick was reduced to mutters and glares. We had ceased arguing long enough to wish Fred a happy birthday and to toast our splendid friendship with the Ferlics. Good thing we were such good friends—Dick and I were not Ozzie and Harriet that night. I was not sure what I was so mad about or exactly what we were arguing about. We usually agreed philosophically on what was right and wrong about sports. I suspected we still agreed, but Dick persisted in wanting to fix it. The year had beaten me down and that night I felt like giving up. I didn't care that much about sports. Let it disintegrate into the quagmire to which it seemed headed. Who cared?

Besides, he was getting on my nerves. As the season progressed he seemed pulled more and more into the vortex of game preparation, traveling, and now this NCAA-impotency frenzy. My patience and my nerves were thin and frayed. I honestly didn't think that I could sit through another basketball game.

I left the Ferlics soon after dinner and drove home. I stopped at our house to pick up the dog and headed straight to the cottage. Exhaustion engulfed me and the car slid precariously over the icy roads. It was a foolish thing to do, but I felt driven by some outside force an irresistible urge to get out of South Bend, to get away by myself, to be alone. The car skidded on icy patches as it zigzagged through the maze of southern Michigan country roads that led to the lake. Tears from the months of tension streamed down my face and obscured my vision. The drive was dangerous and stupid, my head throbbed, and I gasped for air between sobs. My car wound through the last stretch of woods, the bare trees forming a cathedral arch overhead. The cottage was dark, everything was deserted as most of the houses near us on the lake are owned by summer people, like us, who lived elsewhere in the winter. I trudged up the ninety steps, hanging on to the rope railing, slipping on the snow hardened on the steps, my tears freezing on my cheeks. The lake was frozen and forbidding, small hills of ice mixed with sand undulated out into the lake as far as I could see, the lake I loved caught in huge, silent, still waves. My garden had disappeared into the rock-hard earth—the may apples, violets, and columbine mere memories of a happier time.

Inside, the cottage was cold with the heat turned down to 50 degrees and the outside temperature near zero. I drew the drapes and crawled into bed with the quilt pulled up over my head, trying to shut out the world.

Dick called in the morning. "Are you all right?" He knew

where I was, the dog's absence signaled my destination.

"I'm fine but I'm staying up here for a couple of days. I just can't stand it anymore. It's all too goddamned crazy."

"You're not coming in for the game?"

"No. I'm completely out of energy. I can't sit through another game right now. I just want to sleep all day." A little later Jenny called. "Mom, are you okay?"

"I'm fine, Jenny. I just needed to get away for a while. I'm not feeling so great."

"Aren't you coming in for the game?" She couldn't believe I would actually miss a game. Especially not then, when being loyal was so important. I felt guilty, but I knew I could not move from the bed and drive to town.

Karen called. "You're being selfish and self-indulgent," she accused me. "Dad needs you there, he needs all of us." No adequate reply occurred to me.

Dick called again. "I'll come up after the game," he said. "Is that okay? Do you mind?" I was crying again, my emotions running amok. "Sure, it's okay. I'm sorry I'm missing the game. I just can't do it."

I lay on the bed all afternoon with the television changer in my hand and flicked on the game just long enough to get an occasional score. Dick was right about the NCAA. They had an emergency session the night before and reinstated the players, just in time for them to make the plane to South Bend. Syracuse showed up full strength, the players' transgressions forgiven long enough to keep the sponsors happy.

Notre Dame came out in neon green uniforms, a gift from Champion Products, which was trying to promote the new color. Dick loved the green uniform gimmick; it was his idea in 1977 when Dan Devine's Notre Dame football team came out in green uniforms against Southern California. A few years ago, he surprised his players with rather ugly green socks for a big game; the socks met with mixed reviews from the players, but they (the players in the socks) won the game.

Today, the fans went wild, loving or hating the flashy green uniforms, but enthusiastic either way. The atmosphere was like the old days, and the score was close throughout the game. We were ahead by 1 with a few seconds to go when Billy Owens got by now-returned Timmy Singleton for a lay-up. The long pass that failed at the close of the Virginia game succeeded to Daimon Sweet, who was then stripped of the ball—grossly fouled some say—but there was no call and Syracuse hung on to the point win. But it was a moral victory and good old-time Notre Dame basketball.

I knew none of this, of course, as I had only flicked the game on and off, daring to watch only long enough to get the score. When Dick arrived at the cottage, I was still curled in the bed reading a mystery (Adam Dagliesh always made me feel better). It was clear from Dick's face that last night's stress had dropped away from him.

"I think we both overreacted," he began.

"I think so, too. We both needed to blame someone—something—for what's happening. You blame it on the NCAA's failure to clean up college sports; I blame it on you for creating a basketball power at Notre Dame, one that there was no hope of sustaining year after year after year. Not at Notre Dame." I stopped. I was getting worked up again. "I hear I missed a great game." Mary Ferlic and Jenny had both called after the game. Mary was willing to go along with my story that I wasn't feeling well although she suspected that I was really upset about last night. Jenny gave me a play-by-play and made sure I wasn't neglecting the dog.

"God, Terry, I'm exhausted. We worked so hard on that game and we almost had them. It feels good. The kids played great. They listened, they stuck to the game plan, they played their roles almost perfectly. They played their hearts out. It was *fun* today. Did you see the uniforms?"

"Not really. But Mary and Jen told me about them."

"And?"

"Mary thought they were great—she always agrees with your taste. Jenny said they were a *little* bright, but that they got the crowd going. Sounds like the old Digger to me."

The old Digger returned to the office to a letter from the athletic director. Rosenthal said nothing about the game; he wrote only that he was "advised that some time ago we made a decision to stick to our school colors for athletic attire. Regrettably, the wearing of off-color uniforms has raised the issue of the Orange (Syracuse's uniform color) versus the Green, the Protestants versus the Catholics . . . I bring to your attention our policy and ask you to adhere to it in the future." In addition, a memorandum was issued to all head coaches that said that "the policy at this University is for us proudly to wear our school colors, dark blue and gold. . . . Henceforth, only proper uniforms (white trimmed in blue and gold at home and blue and gold on the road) will be acceptable." Dick called me at my law school office to tell me about the responses.

"Very funny. This is a joke, right?"

"Terry, I am dead serious. He really wrote that."

"Doesn't anyone over there have anything important to worry about? No football scandal lately? Come on, you're kidding. Out with it." I started to laugh and Dick started too at his end of the phone. I laughed until tears were streaming down my face. We were choking and out of breath; we were—finally—laughing and laughing and laughing.

16

The poets who wrote that April is the cruelest month had never been to South Bend in February. Nor had they ever suffered through a basketball season. The combination of the two—bitterly cold February, the third month of icy temperatures with no relief in sight, and mid-basketball season when it gets tough to stay optimistic about postseason bids if the season isn't going well and it is too soon to start talking about "next year"—makes February's relatively brief appearance feel endless. Dick and I were at least liking each other more since the release of our laughter after the Syracuse game. We made a running joke of colors reminding us of world problems. "Terry, these carrots in the salad," Dick said one night, "they make me feel bad."

"Huh? It's not often I even make salad these days. Don't criticize."

"Yeah, but—it's this orange and green. It makes me think of the conflict in Ireland."

And every time I saw one of the ubiquitous "Catholics versus Convicts" T-shirts that were so popular among the students—the

shirt referring to the Notre Dame–Miami football series—I wondered why they weren't banned on campus, although they always
made me laugh because they reminded me of the comment made
by an Australian priest who was visiting here last year. "Young
man," he said to a student wearing a "Catholics versus Convicts"
shirt, "in my country, they're the same thing."

I was beginning to find humor in everything. (How else could
I cope with another four-games-in-eight days series? If I dared to
think seriously about that kind of schedule, I got furious.) My
guard was down, which may explain why I agreed to talk to a local
reporter. She called me at my office, saying that she heard that I
was active in feminist concerns at Notre Dame and that the paper
would like to do a story about that. The previous weekend, I
chaired a panel called "The Situation of Women in Various
Professions" at a day-long celebration of women at the Snite
Museum on campus. It was the Year of Women at Notre Dame,
a dubious idea, yet when I had been asked to be on the committee
I agreed, figuring that sensitive input was better than complaining
behind the scenes. The weekend panel included a woman who
worked at the paper, and the local television station covered the
event and interviewed me. I assumed that this was what attracted
the *Tribune*'s attention and prompted the call. The reporter did not
seem to know who my husband was; this would not be what I so
carefully avoided for two decades: a "What the Coach's Wife Is
Like" story. So I said yes.

I learned the hard way that newspaper reporters aren't really
interested in what a coach's wife is like. Instead, they come to you
with a preconceived notion of what kind of story they want and
then they fit you into that. In Dick's first year as a head coach, the
Fordham year, he was attracting a fair amount of press attention.
When a reporter called saying he wanted to do a story on me, I
was flattered. Here was my chance for fame. And like all of us, I
thought I was pretty interesting. I had returned to school at
Fordham that year, as well as raising three small children. In

addition, I regularly did substitute teaching to supplement Dick's $14,000-a-year salary. And I loyally attended all the games. When the reporter arrived at our house in Beacon, New York, I talked about my aspirations, my family, my ambitions, myself. The reporter seemed fascinated. During the interview, I excused myself, explaining that the plumbing in our new house wasn't working well, that the washing machine was backing up all over the basement and I needed to attend to it.

The story appeared two days later. The headline read "Terry Phelps's Real Soap Opera" and it focused on my problems with my washing machine. The reporter wanted a story about a pretty little lovelywife, gallantly coping with domestic emergencies while her husband coaches. And he wrote it. I vowed never again to talk to a reporter.

I had one small lapse the year that Notre Dame made it to the Final Four. Needing to create story after story to hype the event, reporters even resort to interviewing wives. Taken up with the excitement of the event, I agreed to talk to a reporter, temporarily forgetting my vow. All I can recall of the interview is the reporter asking me something about being a female student at Notre Dame. Not given to sound-bite replies, I thought hard about how to answer. "In some ways, I suppose Notre Dame has politicized me," I said. "I'm forced to think about the fact that I'm a woman more than I used to. It's made me something of a feminist." The "Notre Dame politicized me and made me a feminist" part of a lengthy interview appeared in bold print in the *New York Times* and fully obscured any other details of the interview. This reporter wanted controversy, and, forgetting what reporters were like, I delivered.

Another decade had passed and my memory was getting dim. I was vain enough to think that this time the reporter was actually interested in me. When the reporter came to interview me in my office, she began by asking what I taught about women and the law.

"I developed a new course here," I explained. "At Yale Law School two years ago, I studied with Catharine MacKinnon and Judith Resnik, two major feminist legal scholars. MacKinnon has been very involved in the sexual harassment cases and Resnik argued the Rotary Club case at the Supreme Court, one of the cases that required the large service clubs to accept women members. I learned a great deal from both of them—they have quite different approaches—and since Notre Dame did not have a course dealing with these issues, I proposed one." I gave her a copy of my syllabus and she asked if she could attend a lecture I was giving the following week in a colleague's class.

"I don't see why not," I said, a little uncomfortable at the prospect. I tried to keep my coach's wife status and the attention that it generated away from my academic life. It was very difficult for me to establish credibility as a scholar. Coaches' wives, in most academics' minds, are not faculty material. I fought this sub-rosa battle throughout my career as a student and as a teacher. But this occasion seemed to be focused on *my* work, not my coach's wife role. It should be safe. Besides, these issues were important to me and they deserved some publicity.

The reporter quickly burst my bubble. "We'd like the article to come out during basketball season."

"Basketball season? What does that have to do with women and the law?"

She was a little embarrassed. "Well, of course, our readers are interested in the fact that you are Digger Phelps's wife. And that you're doing this kind of work."

So what do I do? Do I end the interview and cancel the story, if indeed I can, because I feel as though I've been misled? Perhaps that's not fair. Perhaps she assumed that I would know that the Digger Phelps's wife part was always of interest. Perhaps she didn't know (how could she?) that I tried to keep my two identities entirely separate. I had begun to like her—a young mother, working part time as a reporter, endeavoring, as I had for so long, to balance competing jobs. I plunged ahead. "All right. No problem. Of course, readers find that interesting."

"If you don't mind," she pressed, "how do you feel about the pressure that's presently on your husband? All the controversy surrounding the losing season?"

I answered; I think on reflection that I answered at some length because I felt that the answer was related to feminism—the kind of feminism that denies the importance of male hierarchies. "Why does it make such a difference," I wondered aloud, "where a team is ranked? Who wins or loses by a point? A better vision of sports is one that looks to what sports does for all of us, how it affects how we relate to each other, what good it brings into our lives. This season, for example, has been a tremendous learning experience for the players, especially watching Monty Williams deal with his finding out that he couldn't play basketball anymore."

"How is he dealing with it?"

"Everyone has pitched in and tried to help—the coaches and the other players. Monty is an unofficial 'assistant coach.' Watch him at a game. He's dressed in a suit, sitting with the coaches, talking to them as a colleague not a player. I really admire him. He's handling something I would have trouble handling. It's those kinds of things that make sports in the college setting a worthwhile enterprise."

"How about the pressure on your private life?"

This was a push but I let it go. "It's always difficult being so recognizable in a town this size. For example, late last fall we went to Rocco's after the law school talent show with some friends, including the law school dean and a University vice-president. We had pizza and beer and a lively conversation about world events. Two weeks later we heard that someone was talking about 'Digger being drunk at Rocco's and solving all the problems of the world instead of concentrating on winning basketball games.' That's not much fun to hear. You start to get paranoid and not want to go out at all. I guess people have always gossiped about us. I know my children have gone through a lot, being talked about at school. I always tell them that you have to take the bad with the good, and being talked about is one of the bad things. I try to remember that, too."

A few days later the reporter came to hear my official lecture. I explained to the students that feminist legal scholars say that we don't have to play by the rules that men have developed, that we can discover other ways of relating to each other and other ways of having law function in our society. More emphasis on responsibility, for example, rather than an emphasis on rights, an emphasis that tends to alienate us from each other. We are all, finally, dependent beings, and perhaps women, because they raise the most dependent among us—children—understand this better than men do.

After the class, during which the reporter took many notes on the lively discussion that followed my remarks, she asked if she could come to my office to fill in a few holes in her notes.

"Sure," I said, energized as always by the students. She followed me to my office where I dumped my papers on my desk and collapsed into my chair. Such a class always exhausted and exhilarated me.

She began tentatively and I was a little puzzled at her hesitancy because we had already spent so much time together and she seemed very relaxed with me. We were trusting each other and it had ceased to feel like a typical interview. "There are a few questions I feel I have to ask you if I'm going to be a good reporter," she began. "But I'm a little embarrassed about them."

My warning lights went on and I hesitated. The tenor of this whole interview had changed and I could feel it. "Such as?"

"Well," she laughed, embarrassed, "how do you react to all the rumors about your husband?"

"Such as?" I echoed myself.

She blushed. "Well, you know, rumors about him going into

bars and berating women, and about him on the golf course, and about him having a wandering eye."

I was in shock but I tried to answer. "People have always gossiped about us. I told you about Rocco's. I have a dozen stories like that. This is more of the same. What can I say?"

After she left, the reality of what had happened set in and I felt thoroughly sick and set up. I felt as though the whole interview had been leading up to those questions and that I had not only misjudged but grievously erred in putting myself in a position to fuel the South Bend gossip machine. How could the reporter have spent all those hours with me, how could she have seen what kind of woman I was and then ask me those questions? How could she have listened to me talk about not playing by the antagonistic rules set up by men and then go right ahead and play by them? After I had come to trust her and had talked so frankly to her? How could I have been so stupid?

I left my office and walked the mile home, tears of rage smearing my mascara. But I had little time to be self-indulgent; I had an important meeting later that afternoon. Normally I loved days when I didn't have to drive to work. It meant the weather was decent, that I had time enough in the morning to walk, that I would be able to leave the office before dark, that I had no errands to run after work. That day, however, it isolated me in my office and gave me nowhere to hide my pain. So I walked home and cleaned my smeared makeup off my face, reapplied it, and returned to the law school. I might feel as though knives were turning in me, but no one else was going to know.

I thought about whether I should mention it to Dick at all. He hardly needed anything else right now, but as soon as he entered the house that evening and sat down at the table with me, I let it all spill out. Now I was a little less angry and mainly feeling stupid and naive. "I think I made a big mistake in talking to the paper," I began.

He laughed at first, our family response to the gossip mill.

(The McFaddens once told us that they heard that Digger came home every night, drank a six-pack, and beat me and the dog. "The dog! Never!" we said.) "What does that possibly have to do with a story about you?" he asked.

"My question, too. That's why I'm so upset about it."

"Terry, you know what reporters are like. Most of them aren't interested in the truth. They're interested in creating controversy. Facts just confuse them."

"But you handle the press so well. You actually seem to enjoy it."

"I was lucky. Those Thursday press luncheons while I was at Penn educated me. You know how Frank Dolson took me under his wing."

"Right. Frank. Is he the last of the reporters with integrity?"

"No, there are a few good guys left, guys who aren't afraid to write the truth. But I don't take most of them seriously. Unfortunately the field is dominated by guys who want to make a quick name for themselves. They're not worth worrying about."

Of course, though, I continued to worry. The next day while I was walking to work I decided to call the paper and see if I could get the story pulled. I felt as though the intentions had been misrepresented from the beginning. After a few calls and reassurance from the reporter's editor that the story *was* supposed to be about me and that I wasn't set up ("I never heard those particular rumors," he said), I gave up. I just should have known better.

The following Saturday morning while the team was in Louisville I was awakened by a call from Sharon. "Terry, have you seen the paper?"

"Oh, God, no," I said. "I'm just getting up." The whole newspaper incident had slipped my mind and I forgot all about the story ever appearing.

"It's a wonderful story. I'm so proud of you. Get out of bed and read it."

It was a wonderful story. It was (mainly) about me. It did not include any gossip. Reading it made me feel good but also was a painful reminder of the way the whole interview ended. It made me understand why I have always been so reluctant to let anyone come close, to know what I'm like, and I suspect it will be a long time before I talk to a reporter again. But if I had to give a title to the whole incident, I'd call it "Terry Phelps's Real Soap Opera."

17

I was sitting on a bar stool in Runyon's in New York City next to Jay Jordan, a Notre Dame alumnus and a good friend. It was February 1991. We had just lost by a point to St. John's—back in the Garden again, my favorite place. Jay, a wonderful fan, was talking about the high points of the game, how well the team played, how close so many of the games have been, and how it hasn't been such a bad year after all. Ever the optimist, he was talking about a possible NIT bid although our record now stood at a grim 12 and 18 (yes, 30 games and February was not yet over). "Yes," he said, responding to my reminding him of the record, "but lots of close games, four losses by three points or less, an incredibly tough schedule with most opponents ranked. It's still possible."

He was trying to cheer me up, but his efforts weren't necessary. I was barely listening to him, letting my mind be taken over by a reverie induced by the twenty year reunion of Dick's Fordham basketball team that was taking place in Runyon's that night.

My mind returned to 1971 after another Notre Dame game; Notre Dame, ranked in the top ten and led by the incomparable Austin Carr, has lost and I am celebrating because we have beaten them.

We? Fordham University, emerging from relative obscurity into the national limelight, in the middle of its best season ever— even twenty years later, it is Fordham's most memorable year. And, in many ways, ours as well.

In the spring of 1970, the annual musical-coaches game began. Dick was finishing his fourth year as an assistant at the University of Pennsylvania. He had accomplished what they, the head coach Dick Harter and his young staff, had set out to do— pull Penn out of the perennial Ivy League and Big Five cellars. Dick had just coached the freshman team to an undefeated season. High school seniors were beginning to take Penn seriously as a potential school—names like Corky Calhoun, Dave Wohl, Craig Littlepage, Bob Morse, and Steve Bilski appeared on the roster. Dick felt he was ready for a head coaching job.

During the four years that Dick spent at Penn, Rick and Jenny were born and I supplemented an assistant coach's salary with occasional substitute teaching—everything from Spanish-speaking kindergartens to high school Latin classes. We finally put enough money together to afford a down payment on our first house and recently celebrated our first anniversary of being home-owners. Then the spring rumors began: Jack Magee was going to leave Georgetown and go to Holy Cross; Jack Donahue was going to leave Holy Cross and go to Fordham. . . . Dick thought he might have a shot at the Georgetown job. But it didn't turn out that way. Dick returned home from the Final Four at Maryland to a message that he should call Pete Carlesimmo, Fordham's athletic director, to talk about the Fordham head basketball coaching position.

He got the job along with what we saw as a stunning salary: $14,000. We felt rich and began to look for a place to live. With three children under five years old, we eliminated the possibility of living in New York City and contacted a realtor in Westchester County. When we told him what we thought we could afford for a house, he laughed. "You can't find a garage in Westchester for that kind of money," we were told. So much for feeling rich; we began to feel naive.

By moving over fifty miles away from Fordham, we were able to find something we could afford, although it meant a long commute for Dick. And also for me, as I hoped to be able finally to return to school. Fordham had thrown in a tuition waiver for me as part of Dick's salary package.

Dick hired Frank McLaughlin, former Fordham star, as his assistant and they went to work. Everyone was returning from a team that had gone 10 and 15 the year before. Dick and Frank hoped, at best, to improve that to a winning season. They also set about to recruit players who would put Fordham basketball on the map.

There were some problems, of course. We lived so far away from the Fordham campus that Dick left before the children were up in the morning and rarely arrived home before they went to bed. Once he arrived home slightly earlier than usual, just after I had settled them in under their covers. "Get up," I called to them. "Come and see Daddy."

"Is he on television again?" Karen asked.

Also among the problems was the head coach's office at Fordham, a basement room, complete with pipes running down a back wall. "This is really going to impress recruits," Dick complained. "How are we ever going to convince them that this is a big-time program?" Recruits, at seventeen years old, often base their decisions on where to go to school on what kind of car the coach drives, or how fancy his office is, or what suits the assistant wears. Dick could hide our two-year-old station wagon, and we could dress Frank up, but the office? No way to hide that.

So I rolled up my sleeves and set to work. I was used to

working wonders with little money and had taught myself to sew, upholster, wallpaper, and repair appliances. I carefully measured the pipe-covered wall in the basement office, bought yards and yards of gold corduroy from a wholesale fabric outlet, and made drapes that lined the wall. With Dick's desk polished and gleaming in front of the drapes, and a few pictures on the wall, the office wasn't bad. Not posh, but not embarrassing.

I'd like to be able to report that the drapes were the reason for Fordham's startling success. But new recruits were not responsible for Fordham's most memorable year. Instead it was the very players who were already there, the same ones who had fumbled their way to a 10 and 15 season, the ones I could so easily identify, even in a darkened bar twenty years later. A little grayer, a little heavier, only a few years younger than we were as we all drifted into middle age within a few years of each other: Charlie Yelverton, Tom Sullivan, Bill Mainor, Jack Burik, George Zambetti, Bart Woytowitz, Tom Pipich, Steve Kane, Bob Larbes, and twelfth-man P. J. Carlesimmo (who's done pretty well for himself since as head coach at Seton Hall). Only Kenny Charles was missing from the reunion.

The memory of the Fordham year now floats like a tranquil island in a turbulent sea. Ah, nostalgia. It was anything but tranquil. The season began predictably enough with a win over Yale; but then win after win occurred over teams which comprise the present-day Big East: Boston College, Syracuse, Seton Hall, St. John's, Pittsburgh, Georgetown, and Connecticut—along with wins over Army (coached by Bobby Knight, who, in response to a fan saying, "Tough loss, Coach," after the game, snapped back, "All losses are tough!"), Rutgers, and a single loss to Temple.

Dick was not only head coach; he was head cheerleader, band director, captain of the pep squad. He encouraged the formation of a pom-pom squad called the Ramettes and urged them to do a routine to the then-popular "All Right Now." He coached the players into a 32-minute pressing game that teams in that part of the country hadn't tried before and he convinced the players that they could beat anybody with it. P. J. Carlesimmo organized a pep rally in a dorm before the season began and Jackie Burik, addressing the students, loudly proclaimed, "We're gonna win with this press!" Students jammed the tiny Rosehill Gymnasium, rocked to the music, and cheered on their miracle-making team. All of New York City watched with stunned admiration and even people off the Fordham campus began to sport "Digger" buttons. Rookie *Sports Illustrated* writer Larry Keith wrote an article called "Love Story on Rosehill," about the city's infatuation with the team, playing off the fact that part of the popular movie *Love Story* had been filmed at Fordham. Fordham was the city's team and everyone loved this bunch of former losers who ran, pressed, played way over their heads, and beat nearly everyone.

The Notre Dame–Fordham game in Madison Square Garden was the first college basketball sellout in years. Since that year, I have met scores of people who tell me that they were at that game: it was a kind of watershed experience for many basketball fans. Notre Dame was having a great year with the Washington, D.C., trio of Austin Carr, Collis Jones, and Sid Catlett leading the way. They were ranked in or near the top ten and despite Fordham's impressive record, no one really believed that Fordham had a prayer. (Speaking of prayers, Jackie Burik's mother took care of that for the Fordham players as she sprinkled them with holy water before every game.)

The holy water, or perhaps it was Billy Mainor taking over after Charlie Y fouled out with 7 minutes left in the game, worked its miracle that night. Or perhaps it was the zone defense for the first 30 minutes of the game (Notre Dame had lost 5 out of 6 games to zones) that converted to a man-to-man press for the final 10 minutes of the game. Whatever it was, Fordham came away with a win in front of 19,500 fans who had witnessed a game few would forget. After the game as Dick and I, carrying the game ball, walked to Gallagher's for a postgame celebration, cars stopped in the street and their drivers emerged to shake Dick's hand. "Great game, Coach!" "Way to go, Digger!" rang in our ears. It seemed as though that night all of New York City had watched the scrappy Fordham players and their young coach pull off an exquisite upset. Even the subway alumni abandoned Notre Dame, suddenly realizing, or so it seemed, that Fordham was full of Irish Catholics, too.

Headline writers began to have a field day with the name "Digger": "Fordham Digs Past ND"; "The 'Digger' Deals Death Blow to Foes of Ram's Undertakings"; "Phelps Digs Up Frenzy at Fordham." Any secret hope I had fostered that the "Digger" nickname would disappear soon after college was deep sixed forever.

A week after the victory over Notre Dame, Marquette (Dean "the Dream" Meminger, Jim Chones, Allie McGuire and Company), coached by Allie's dad, Al McGuire, and ranked third in the country, came into the Garden to play Fordham. Early that day, before Dick left for the fifty-three-mile (not that we were counting!) drive to Fordham, I noticed his flushed face and glistening eyes, more dramatic than a usual "game-face" transformation. "Are you feeling okay?" I asked. "You look like you have the flu or something."

"I do feel pretty lousy. Do you think I have a fever?"

I searched out a thermometer which revealed that Dick was indeed running a 102 temperature. Then I asked perhaps the most naive question in my career as a coach's wife. "Are you going to go in? You can't coach with a fever that high!"

Dick did not dignify my question with an answer. He merely gave me an incredulous look, reached for his coat, and started for the door. "See you after the game," he said.

Again in front of a record second sold-out house, the Fordham players put in a memorable, statistic-defying performance. When Charlie Y blocked Jim Chones's first shot into the fifth row,

19,500 fans stood up to cheer and never sat down again. Marquette was only able to pull out a win in overtime. Al McGuire also put in a memorable performance, pacing the sidelines, riding the refs, controlling the game's tempo. By the game's end, he had the refs eating out of the palm of his hand, or completely intimidated. In any case, you could be pretty sure that late game calls would go Marquette's way. After the game, Dick, still feverish, said that he would never let that happen to him again. He would never let the other coach get control of the refs as Al had done. And I would never, ever, again ask him if he was not going to coach because he was sick. And he never, ever, missed a game for the next twenty years.

By season's end, Fordham had won 25 games and had received an NCAA bid, its first in years. It was the tournament's Cinderella team and no one was very surprised or disappointed when they lost in the second round to Villanova in Raleigh, North Carolina. Fordham's final record was 26 and 3 and the name *Digger Phelps* was on the mind of every athletic director looking for a new coach. Offers began pouring in. Dick flew to Blacksburg, Virginia, where the president of VPI met him at the airport. The Penn job opened and Dick was offered the chance to go back as head coach and coach the great players he had been so instrumental in recruiting. And then the Notre Dame head basketball coaching job became vacant. The rest, as they say, is history.

The New York press, feeling jilted, raked Dick over the coals for breaking his three-year contract with Fordham and going to Notre Dame. I compulsively bought all three New York papers every day and combed the sports pages to see what was being said. One writer accused Dick of opportunism and suggested that he would pick up and leave Notre Dame after a short stay. The public criticism, my first experience of it, stung like nettles and I wrote responses in my head. But Dick ignored it all and never once doubted that he had made the right decision. Fordham fans and alumni never forgave him for turning his back on their school.

Whenever we played Fordham in the Garden or shared the Garden with Fordham, the Fordham students carried signs deriding Dick for leaving. "You weren't even born when I left!" Dick sometimes yelled back at them.

Twenty years later that wonder team has come together for a reunion. It many ways it was a perfect year: singular, unrepeatable, unforgettable, a high point in all our lives. No one expected anything; no demands were made. It was a gift, a wonderful surprise, and even twenty years later, we all still wonder at it. How did they do it? How did it happen? No one dares to probe too deeply. They did do it. It did happen. That's enough. No one stayed around too long to disappoint raised expectations.

As the former Fordham players reminisce after the St. John's–Notre Dame game, they fall back into the roles they played as teammates: the leaders, the pranksters, the quiet ones, the talkers—they're still the same. I'm beginning to understand better what sports does, what it stands for in people's lives. It captures moments, it captures the past as nothing else quite does.

During our first year at Notre Dame, we attended a banquet after a football game, a reunion of one of Frank Leahy's great postwar teams. Leahy was sick, dying actually at the time, and could not attend. But he spoke to his former players over the telephone and his feeble, frail voice was amplified by microphone for all of us to hear. A former player sitting near me, a man well into middle age, wept openly, remembering his respect and affection for his coach. He and his teammates joined in the old Notre Dame chant for Leahy: "He's a man, he's a man, he's a Notre Dame man," their highest form of praise. Their moments as players were real, alive, immediate again. In some ways, you can go home again. Home is where, when you go there, they remember who you were.

And so it is tonight. Tommy Sullivan, still handsome but graying, now P. J.'s assistant at Seton Hall, tells me how upset he and P. J. get over rumors that Dick is leaving Notre Dame, possibly getting fired, and that P. J. might replace him as Notre Dame's basketball coach. "They don't understand what Digger means to us," he says. "He was our *coach*. He gave us one of the best years of our lives."

18

In *The Trial* by Franz Kafka, Joseph K. awakened one morning to find that he was arrested although he was not told what his crime was. As my students tried to unravel this surreal existential novel, we decided that Joseph K.'s crime, or fatal flaw, was that he tried to make sense of the events that have happened to him. One of Kafka's points, a student argued cogently, is that life does not make sense, that there are no reasons for what happens to us. We struggle daily to find order, to discover meaning, only finally to die understanding nothing, just as Joseph K. does.

And so at the end of a Kafkaesque year, we traveled to Chicago, the city of big shoulders, to play the last game of the season, perhaps our last game ever, against DePaul. In the years before the architectural horror known as the Rosemont Horizon was built, we played DePaul in the old Alumni Gym on DePaul's campus, a classic "pit," deep in the heart of the north side of Chicago. It was a bandbox, with seats virtually on the floor, the stands jammed with DePaul students and fans hot for Notre Dame blood. An organ with its volume far too loud for the size of the gym blasted out something that I suppose was music—it only sounded like more noise, joining the screaming fans' voices into an earsplitting cacophony. It was a tough place to play, the kind of place that Dick loved and I dreaded. Continued cries of "Sit down, Digger" only revved up his coaching engine.

When Karen was thirteen, I gave her a special treat of a trip with the team to Chicago for the DePaul game. We would spend some good mother–daughter time together during the day and attend the game at night. That night when we entered Alumni Gymnasium, I realized that my plan was not a perfect one. I held tightly to her hand as the crowd pushed up against her slender frame. But she had been attending basketball games since she was a year old and despite the noise and the crowd her eyes beamed. For a while. Shortly into the game, Dick, as was his habit, stood and paced, yelling instructions at the team and side comments at the referees. As usual, he performed rather than suffered through a basketball game. He had inherited the performance mantle (or black cloak, depending on your perspective) from Al McGuire, the now-retired black knight of college coaching. He dared the crowd to get on him, hoping to distract them from getting on his players. The DePaul crowd cooperated: "Digger, sit down. Digger, sit down."

"Are they yelling at Dad?" Karen asked.

"Yes, honey, they always do. It doesn't mean anything; it's actually kind of funny."

The crowd shifted its chant. "Digger, go home. Digger, go home."

"Mom, they're telling my dad to go home." By now Karen was crying, my explanation ignored. "Don't they like him? He can't go home, they have to finish the game."

"It's just for fun, Karen. They don't mean it." I put my arm around her to comfort her, but felt her shoulders shake with sobs. I decided that my accounting for the crowd's taunts was not convincing her and I needed to get her out of there. I'd been at DePaul games before. Things weren't going to get any better. "Come on, let's go to the ladies' room."

Once away from curious eyes, Karen's crying took over and she sobbed long and hard. "Listen, Karen," I began. "This is a basketball arena, and in here isn't reality. Real life stops when you walk through the door. Ordinary people yell things and do things they would never do anywhere else."

"I don't. I'm the same."

"Yes, but . . ." Words failed me. I didn't even believe what I was saying. I didn't understand it much better than Karen did. I understood that it was partly entertainment, part of a big show of some sort. Moreover, Karen's father was complicitous in it. I had gotten used to it and, unlike Karen, I didn't cry. But its significance, its justification, eluded me, had always eluded me. I could live with it but I couldn't explain it. And I worried over what lessons we teach our children by justifying it. What horror show transformation happened to the ordinary person when he passed through the turnstiles? The stands often seemed filled with Mr. Hydes and werewolves and vampires, out for gore and blood, ranting under the lights as if the lights were so many full moons.

Despite the obvious rancor of the crowd, the Notre Dame–DePaul rivalry had always been a good one, one that we enjoyed through the years. DePaul is, in many ways, a city version of Notre Dame. It's an urban Catholic school that educated thousands of first-generation Catholic immigrants—many in its night school. Notre Dame came into the picture when these men became successful and moved to the suburbs. With newfound wealth and position in the community, they sent their sons to Notre Dame.

Beyond this natural affinity, Dick and DePaul's longtime coach, Ray Meyer, always had a close relationship. Ray was a father figure to Dick, a venerable, experienced coach when Dick was new in the game. Ray had been at DePaul for thirty years, some lean and some successful, his long tenure at DePaul an impressive testament to DePaul's commitment to a dedicated coach. Some of Ray's most successful teams came when we too were at a peak in the late seventies. I recall a bittersweet moment when we had just beaten DePaul in the NCAA tournament to advance to the Final Four. It was a wonderful time for us, a dream come true, but as we waited for the team in Lawrence, Kansas, after the game, I saw Marge Meyer, Ray's wife, also waiting for her team with tears of disappointment in her eyes. Ray, like most coaches, had been criticized for "not winning the big one," and I'm sure she envisioned a renewed chorus of critics. All over a point or two, the serendipity of whether a last shot falls or bounces off the rim. If it falls, you're a genius; if it bounces off, you're a fool. Fans choose to see it as coaching. My sympathy for Marge, a woman I had long admired, mitigated my own joy at having finally been lucky enough to win the big one. Marge was a coach's wife in the old mold. She loved basketball and probably knew as much about it as Ray did. She voluntarily attended Chicago high school games and scouted talent for her husband. Although I wouldn't have emulated her for all the world, I saw her as a trouper and a great woman. Oh, damn, I remember thinking. Why did we have to beat *them?* Why couldn't we both go?

The move to the Horizon has not mellowed the DePaul crowd, only made it larger and raised the noise level as planes bound to and from O'Hare Airport buzz frighteningly close to the domed roof. I swore off games in the Horizon several years ago, but this year it was important that I be there. I traveled to Chicago with Mary and Fred Ferlic earlier in the day, and we met up with John and Mary Houck and Brian and Sharon Regan in Ricardo's, John's favorite Chicago restaurant. After dinner Dick, having come later on the team bus, joined us at a club near the hotel to listen to Buddy Charles, the best piano player in Chicago according to Tex. The strain of the year was showing on Dick, he looked old, a little beaten, and I had sometimes been startled when I had seen him on television. The camera seemed to emphasize the fatigue on his face, and I found myself worrying a little about his health.

These friends, though, were loyal, stalwart even, in the face of this grim year. We told them nothing of the inside machinations of the University and it was hard to tell how much they guessed. I could tell how concerned they were for us, though, and I was touched by the gentleness with which they kidded Dick in an attempt to lighten his mood. They are enthusiastic about sports, but with a measured approach, aware that these are, first of all, *students,* averaging about twenty years old. They seem to realize how difficult it is to have one's well-being riding on the backs of teenagers, who, despite their unusual talent on the basketball court, have all the same problems and insecurities as do teenagers everywhere.

We ended the evening early. Dick, after all, had to work the following day. Neither of us had slept well for months, and that night before the DePaul game was no exception. After a few hours of fitful sleep, I plunged deep into a bottomless dream. I was attending a function at Notre Dame at which I had some official role to play. The huge room was filled with men, dressed in either gray suits and white shirts or black suits with white collars. My role, it seemed, was to approach each one and inquire something of him. I would walk up to each man and put out my hand and say, "I'm Terry Phelps." And each man would reply enthusiastically, "Of course, how nice to see you, Terry," and shake my hand or kiss me. Then I would say, "I need to ask you why . . ." Before I ever got to the end of the question, a film covered the man's face, obscuring his features, and he turned away humming part of the Notre Dame Fight Song in a monotone: "While our loyal sons are marching," or "Shake down the thunder from the sky," or some other phrase, repeating it over and over. I dashed from man to man desperately trying to reach the end of my question, but each time the same thing happened and the room was now filled with the sound of various verses, repeated and repeated with no tune, like a chant. It was like something from *Invasion of the Body Snatchers,* when people you think you know seem possessed by aliens, turned into creatures who cannot respond to you. I began to realize that I was dressed in a shocking red dress and that I stood out like a stalk of orphan corn in this field of gray and black. But I could not stop, the room seemed filled with an infinite number of men to whom I must speak. Some waking part of my consciousness pulled me, ripped me, out of the dream, and I hung for a moment between the dream and waking. I heard Dick murmur, "Terry, are you asleep?"

"No. I had the most dreadful dream. Can't you sleep either?"

"I need to talk to you. I've been lying here for hours thinking about the Syracuse weekend, about what I love about coaching and what I've come to hate about it. I've decided not to try to coach next year. I'm quitting, getting out, retiring from basketball."

I, for once, had nothing to say. I knew that his tone was not inviting conversation, it had a finality that I had not heard before. I pulled myself out of the bed and turned away, studying the sham Japanese print on the wall, its colors blurring through my tears. "Give up? Not fight?"

"Terry, enough's enough. Look at next year's schedule—sixteen road games. No coach can succeed if he has no say over the schedule. The travel alone will kill us. And with no University support, the public speculation will never end and will constantly drain energy away from the team. Look at what the response has been to questions about my future. 'We review every coach every year.' After twenty years of opening my veins for Notre Dame, I'm to be 'reviewed.' When adversity hit us, when we lost three players this year, the University turned its back on us. I've had enough."

"How can you leave next year's team to someone else? You have four starters returning, LaPhonso should be able to stay eligible in his senior year, and the new recruits are ranked as one of the top classes in the country. You *know* you can win twenty games, even with that killer schedule. They won't have the nerve to fire you. I know they won't."

"I just don't want to face them down. I guess they've worn me out. You were right, you know. I can't fix everything. It doesn't mean enough to me anymore to go through it."

"But none of this makes any sense. If coaches like you are driven out of the game by this kind of pettiness, by people too small to stand up for anything, by people who care only about making money, what's going to happen to college basketball?"

"I can't fight college basketball's battles anymore. I've tried, I've spoken out, made myself unpopular. I need to get on with my life. I want to put basketball behind me."

I felt like Joseph K. in *The Trial*, impaired with the need for reasons, with the need to make sense of life, to make sense of the past year. I would not have given in; I would have gone down in the burning plane. But we weren't talking about me. I wasn't the one who had to stand alone in front of hostile crowds, who had to work on a daily basis for people whose values were so foreign from mine. I wasn't the one who had to face reporters who asked questions about the deafening silence coming from Notre Dame officials. Perhaps most of all, I wasn't the one who promised recruits and their parents an education and then was forced to play a schedule that precluded that possibility. I understood that Dick felt he had no options left coaching Notre Dame basketball. Anything that he could do, that he had, in fact, done in the past to regain his earlier success had been taken out of his hands. His hands were more than tied, they were, essentially, cut off.

And to be honest, I had noticed a change in his coaching in the last few games. Sure, he was overwhelmingly tired and that showed. But it was more than fatigue. Some hope, some optimism, that craziness that made him practice cutting down the nets before the 1974 UCLA game, that made him hitch rides on snow plows to get to practice, that constant belief that his team, no matter what the statistics said, could beat anybody, all that hadn't exactly disappeared but seemed to beat more faintly, like the heart of a stubborn dying man, pulsing slowly, ever more slowly, its life ebbing away. There was an energy he had always infused into his teams, the unseen ingredient that pushed them so often over the top, the ingredient that great coaches had and mediocre ones did not. That energy was missing. He didn't know it; or if he had noticed something wrong, he believed it was just temporary. And perhaps it was. But some part of me knew that under the reigning circumstances, there was little hope of it returning.

The opened drape revealed a black sky, that interlude between late night and pre dawn when the stars have shut down but daylight has not yet come. A black city sky, glowing faintly orange. I longed to lay my throbbing heard on Chicago's big shoulders and sleep for a long time. Reality confronted me—hard—and unfortunately would not let me hide behind my own carefully thought out propositions. I'd managed to smile through twenty-five years of coaching. Could I possibly smile through this, too? This giving in to all that was wrong with college sports, this surrender? I felt suspended between past and future. Between my life as a coach's wife and my life after.

I waited a few moments, struggling to regain control. At last I turned my dry-eyed face to Dick. "Okay. If that's what you want, I'm with you."

19

The spring thaw had come at last. Although the weather wouldn't be warm until May, the snow finally melted except for the biggest drifts and the huge piles created by the snow plows. Brave early bulbs were beginning to poke through the still-hard ground near our front door.

It's true about letting go. Now that the decision was made, we relaxed into plans for the future. I decided to direct the Notre Dame Law Centre in London from January to June 1992—thousands of miles away from Notre Dame basketball. Rumors were widespread nationally and locally about whether Dick would resign or be fired or even stay on. We said nothing. The press was relentless; one reporter tracked us down in our hotel room the morning after the DePaul game. "Digger," she said, "the hot rumor in New York is that you're resigning and P. J. is getting the job. Is that true?" I peered at the clock and could not believe that it was only 7 A.M. and a reporter had called. How dreary to be somebody, I thought, aided by Emily Dickinson. How public, like a frog.

Dick received letter after letter asking him to hang on, not to quit. Another coach at Notre Dame wrote, "Those of us who coach really appreciate what you have done for all of us. Keep up the good work, circle the wagons, and things will be fine." I slowly realized how much Dick was carrying around for all of us, how his hanging in there symbolized hope for the future of sports at Notre Dame—that it was possible to do it the right way. I began to understand, too, how unfair this was to him, that I, as much as anyone, wanted him to be the one who stood up for all of us. An English professor I scarcely knew stopped me in the library: "Tell Digger that many of us are behind him. We're not much for writing letters to the paper or calling in the sports talk shows, but what he has done here means a lot to us." I tried to smile in response. "Thanks. I really appreciate your saying that. I'll tell him." What I didn't say what that it was too late. Another close friend saw me on campus. "Terry, I know what you and Dick are going through, but don't make any hasty decisions. I don't know what Dick is planning to do. I don't even know all of what's gone on this year, although I've heard hints and rumors. I've got it from a good source that the University is going to back down; they're not going to fire Dick. They've finally come to realize that firing Dick will be a major public relations disaster. Besides, a couple of major donors have gotten wind of what's happening here and are threatening to withdraw their money. It's probably none of my business and I shouldn't be telling you this, but I love you both. And I know you're both in pain."

Terrific, I thought. All it took was money. We should have thought of that a year ago. But I was silent for a moment, my silence paying tribute to this extraordinary friend. Out loud I said, "Things have really gone a bit too far if that's happening. We'll be okay. Don't worry about us."

Joe Haggar called from Dallas to talk to Dick. Joe is an alumnus from a family that has given a great deal of money and support to both Saint Mary's and Notre Dame. He was one of the kindest people I knew, calling after losses in particular, year after year, to give Dick pep talks. His calls were so regular that when the phone rang after a particularly tough game, I was sure it was Joe—and it usually was. "What's this I'm hearing?" he asks me in his fetching Texas drawl. "You tell Dick he's not leaving Notre Dame. This is just a down year, we all have slumps. No running away. He'll come back, I know it."

"Thanks, Joe. I'll pass that on to Dick. I'm sure he'll call you before he does anything. Give our love to Isabel."

Our friend Ken Hoffman, president of Hart/Marx, took us to dinner in Chicago. "Look," he said, "you can't start second-guessing yourself. You haven't gotten to where you are, you haven't won all those games, because you don't know what you're doing. It happens in business all the time. You have a bad quarter, or even a bad year. Trust what you've accomplished. Trust that you know what you're doing. You'll bounce back."

"Hard to bounce when someone's taken all the air out of the ball," Dick said and changed the subject.

We heard gossip, rumor, innuendo, and we were soul-sick and bone-tired. It was too late. The decision made in that Chicago hotel room was irrevocable. There was no going back. It was too long and too hard to get to it and neither of us was willing to reopen the issue. My own disappointment at abandoning the fight was giving way to immense relief. Notre Dame basketball would go on without us.

I had my last nightmare about basketball. Notre Dame was playing a basketball game and I arrived late, after the game had begun. Dick was sitting on a center bench on the floor, alone, and I sat down next to him. We were playing a big game—perhaps Syracuse—and the score was close at the end. Syracuse was a point ahead and they had the ball at their end of the court. Dick did nothing. I turned to him in amazement, "Why don't you have your players foul?"

He replied calmly, "It will all be over in two weeks. Why

worry about it?" Suddenly there was a tussle over the ball and it should be a jump ball, but it took the referees a long time to make the call. They finally called the jump and it was our turn for possession. We dribbled down the court and scored to win.

Since the season had ended (except in my dreams), we had only one more official function, the annual basketball banquet, to undergo. Normally the banquet occurred before the season was over in that for seventeen of the twenty years here we had gone to a postseason tournament. This year, however, there was no tournament bid and since the banquet was the first day of spring break, I scheduled a trip to Key West for Dick, Jenny, Karen, and me the day after the banquet. I was hoping that Dick would get some rest and recover from the ordeal of the past year. I was hoping to distract him from his intense disappointment that this, his last year, turned out so poorly. He deserved better; he certainly deserved to have it end better.

The banquet, as usual, brought out all my neuroses, symbolized by my obsession over what to wear. Usually oblivious to clothes, I become fixated on them when I feel most insecure, when I have an uncomfortable role to play. At the basketball banquet, more than any other time, I was the lovelywife. I rummaged through my closet, trying on dress after dress, discarding them in heaps on the floor. Nothing seemed right and I wished that I had taken the time to shop for something new. I put on a black wool dress with a choker of twisted pearls. No. I looked like a priest and given my involvement with the ordination-of-women committee, people would think I did it on purpose (of course they wouldn't, but my paranoia was high). I tried a wool suit. No. I looked like I had just come from the office. I finally settled on a shocking pink dressy suit, each piece a slightly different shade of pink. It was quite unlike anything I usually wore and I couldn't even remember why I bought it. But that night I was quite unlike myself.

Likewise, the Notre Dame basketball banquets were quite

unlike most sports banquets. They used to be traditional enough, with Dick calling in various chits to get speakers—Al McGuire, even Senator Bill Bradley. But it became clear that the players were the most interesting parts of the banquets. It was the players people came to see and hear, not a speaker, however eminent.

The players were assigned to give the various awards to each other—most valuable player, best rebounder, most improved, and so forth. In giving the awards the players took the opportunity to get in a few humorous digs, not unlike the Christmas gift exchanges. And in receiving awards, the players took the opportunity to give eloquent and moving speeches. It was wonderful to watch frightened and inarticulate freshmen flower into self-assured raconteurs as upperclassmen. Even I rarely got through a banquet without wet eyes—from laughing as well as crying. So we dispensed with the speakers and let the players run the show. And what shows they put on. I sat at the raised head table in the basketball arena, looking down on the circular tables set on the covered basketball floor on which I had seen so much occur in twenty years. I had watched players and their parents come and go. My mental eye saw Mrs. Tripuka with her cow bell, Mr. Salinas, Mr. Branning, the Kemptons, the Hanzliks, the Paxsons, and Adrian Dantley's beautiful, strong mother who insisted after Adrian gave up his senior year to play professional basketball that he return summers to complete his degree. And he did. God, how these people had enriched my life!

Now the gaiety and humor were overshadowed by a somber tone that my shocking pink suit could not brighten. Dick Rosenthal and Father Beauchamp spoke for a combined eighteen minutes without once mentioning Dick's name. "Perhaps you should introduce yourself to them," I whispered. "Apparently they think this team does not have a coach." I began to feel that I was present at a funeral, listening to a eulogy in which the deceased's name was not heard. It was bizarre, surreal almost. More than that, it was needlessly hurtful. They'd won. They have all the power. They get to hire their own basketball coach. Why rub it in?

Their words, as well as their silences, helped me to appreciate better how Dick had been feeling all year. Where he had been confident, cocky even, aggressive, ambitious, a weariness had set in. Even when the old self briefly reappeared—as it had for the Syracuse game—it was so quickly slapped down that it could no longer thrive, perhaps even survive, in such a constrained environment. A disbelieving part of himself had been brought to life. I could see it so clearly now. I was not sure he saw it so explicitly, but he was beginning to believe in his unworthiness, to embrace this negative view of himself. His spirit was dying. What could he do in the face of this? What more did I dare ask of him?

I tried to keep my mind blank and not listen to them. As my mind wandered searching for something to think about, a sudden memory came back, a story I hadn't thought about in years. When we first arrived at Notre Dame, we heard a story that we assumed was apocryphal. "If Knute Rockne had not gone down in that plane," some old townspeople told us, "he would have been fired in a few years. No coach has ever left here under pleasant circumstances. They get bigger than the school and they have to go." We laughed.

After the banquet we gathered with our friends at the University Club for what Dick and I knew was the last time. We ordered the usual pitchers of beer. "Can you believe those s.o.b.'s never mentioned Dick's name?" someone said. So I was not the only one who noticed. It felt strange to have nothing to do after the banquet. In the tournament years, Dick would not even appear at the club. He would be with his assistants, watching tapes, even after the banquet, preparing for the next game. And I would be rushing to pack so I could go along, always taking along a huge pile of student papers, nearly always grading Moot Court briefs in airports and hotel rooms.

Relieved as I was, I felt a little empty. I sensed an absence, something forever gone. I was beginning to understand what Al McGuire meant—"One day you're on top of the world, the next day you're playing handball with the curb. I miss the highs and lows most of all." This had certainly been a "handball with the curb" year, but it was also emotionally intense. Could it be that I'd miss that most of all?

PART FIVE

SPRING

1991

. . . she suddenly began again. "Then it really *has* happened, after all! And now, who am I? I *will* remember, if I can! I'm determined to do it!" But being determined didn't help her much. . . .

—*Through the Looking Glass*

20

My life as a coach's wife at Notre Dame was framed by two press conferences. In 1971, I went with Dick to South Bend for the press conference announcing his accepting the Notre Dame job. I was twenty-six years old and a little overwhelmed by all the attention. I bought a new dress to wear for the press conference—blue and gold, of course. After our first night at the Morris Inn on campus with the glow of the Golden Dome the only rival for the glow in our eyes, I arrived at breakfast to discover that I had been set up with a real estate agent to look at houses all day. I was not expected, not permitted, to attend the press conference. Men talked about sports; their wives looked for houses.

Two decades later, I told Dick that I wanted to be present at the press conference when he announced his retirement. "Why on earth would you want to be there?" he asked.

"This was my decision, too. I want to attend." I go; I don't wear blue and gold.

Just an hour before the Monday press conference, I met my

Law and Literature class. We were discussing Pete Dexter's novel *Paris Trout,* in which the deranged and corrupt Paris has cold-bloodedly shot two black women. The one who did not die, Mary McNutt, testifies at his trial. When Paris's lawyer, Harry Sea-graves, tries to impeach Mary, she replies, "I told the truth about it. You can make it look any which way now, but I told how it happened." Seagraves responds that the jury will decide what happened. Mary says, "They don't decide what happened. It's already done. All they decide is if they gone to do something about it."

Sportswriters, seeking out a truth to their liking, filled the room. From the same scenario each would create his or her own reality. Jenny cut her classes to be present and Karen, now visibly pregnant, flew in from St. Louis where Jamie had begun his season with the Cardinals. Rick was busy giving interviews about his own breaking story about his father's retirement. Dick had written out his remarks, and he began, his hand shaking slightly:

After twenty years as head basketball coach at the University of Notre Dame, I am retiring.

In 1965 I wrote Ara Parseghian explaining my love for Notre Dame and my desire to coach there someday. Little did I know that my dream would become a reality six years later. Every day, even with the ups and downs, has been like Christmas morning opening the presents you always wanted. . . .

Two nights earlier at our lake cottage, Dick sat down with a legal pad and wrote out the speech, beginning to end, straight through. He wrote the way he painted, no censors, no filter. And just as he had called me from my computer to admire his latest painting-in-progress, he called me from my work to read his retirement speech. The elegance, the purity, the fairness he showed amazed me. "I would not have been so nice," I said wryly. And it's true. The speech I would have written would have been adequate—just that, not fresh and honest as Dick's was. I would have carefully chosen my words, searched out double meanings, tried to say things between the lines. I would have gotten it all wrong.

The next day, Sunday, the phone rang early and we discovered that news of the press conference and Dick's announcement has somehow leaked. The phone rang intermittently with calls from the few sportswriters who knew how to reach us at the cottage. I fielded all the calls and said that Dick was not available. One call came from our son, Rick, and Dick asked him, "Are you calling as our son or as the sports editor?"

"The sports editor," Rick replied. "Can I ask you a few questions?" He interviewed his dad and with our permission released the story, the best scoop of his young career.

Dick had planned to tell his assistants on Monday morning, but he decided to return to town early and meet with them that night. The assistants were his only regret; his retirement left them potentially without jobs. Fran McCaffery left a head coaching job at Lehigh to become an assistant at Notre Dame; Matt Kilcullen and his wife, Mary Jo, had a new baby. They met at our house that night—Matt and Mary Jo, Fran, Jeff, Skip (the trainer), Roger Valdiserri, and John Heisler (the sports information director)—ostensibly to discuss the next day's press conference. The discussion developed into a party, a celebration of sorts, a ritual, a way to end it all. Mary Jo and I curled up with our glasses of champagne in the living room while the rest of them told endless stories of past games, trips, players. Outside it thundered, another South Bend spring storm that made me think of *King Lear*.

"All things considered," Mary Jo asked me, "would you do it again?" Matt had just interviewed for the head job at Jacksonville University, and I knew that beneath Mary Jo's question was her anxiety, her fear for her own future.

I was too tired and I had drunk too much champagne. I searched for something wise to tell her and came up blank. "Just bloom where you're planted," I finally said.

Father Beauchamp and Rosenthal were not present at the press conference. Nor was there any offical representative from the University; no gold watch, no balloon bouquet, not even a thank-you note. The athletic director issued a terse four-line statement: "We wish Digger all the best in his new endeavors, whatever they might be. If anyone can appreciate and understand a person opting for a new career, it would be me. The renewal I've found in my new assignment has been a special joy for me and my family, and I wish the same to him." It raised a few eyebrows, but not mine. I found it a fitting symbol of the events of the past few years.

Mary Ferlic grabbed me afterwards with tears in her eyes. She was taking this harder than I was. "How about if I pick up a cake and some champagne and we get together tonight? I'll call the Houcks, the Links, the Regans. Anyone else?" At first this need to celebrate surprised me until I saw that our friends needed closure too. Some era in their own lives was also ending; they had been so much a part of our lives—the wins, the losses, all of it.

"Sure, Mary. Dick and I have been preparing for this for a long time. I feel only relief that it is finally over, that we can get on with our lives."

"But it's new for us. We need to know you're all right."

My tears matched hers and I was deeply touched. We were never alone. There was never any need to worry.

That night it stormed and I dreamed that enormous waves broke off Lake Michigan and pounded against the windows of the cottage. In years past, when the house was threatened by erosion, I used to dream regularly that it fell into the lake, often with me in it. But those dreams ceased long ago. The dream returned and in it the lake rose up and threatened to engulf us. I was not frightened though. I knew it was a dream, that I would awaken and the lake, however angry, would be below, and the cottage, however rain-swept, would be safe.

EPILOGUE:

FROM LONDON,
1992

I am sitting in a bar (is this becoming a theme?)—actually it's a pub called The Goat just around the corner from the London Law Centre. The students and I have surprised Dick with a going-away party (they call it a "leaving party" over here). It is late February and I have been in London since New Year's Day when I started my stint as the director of the law program. I have a flat in Covent Garden, just two blocks away from where Professor Henry Higgens first set eyes on Eliza Doolittle as she sold her flowers outside the Royal Opera House.

Dick joined me for the past six weeks, but now is returning to the States to be a CBS analyst for the NCAA tournament throughout March. After the tournament, he will begin a job as special assistant to former governor Bob Martinez, the drug czar. He is part of a program called "Weed and Seed" that will provide federal help to inner-city neighborhoods that want to clean up their drug-infested streets and start new, alternative activities for the neighborhood children.

My students have given Dick a dart board as a leaving gift and he is making a short speech. "I'm really looking forward to Washington," he says. "I know the cities are a mess, I've been recruiting in them for twenty-five years. I know some people think that it's too late, that nothing can be done. But I say, 'So what if you're 20 points down at the half? You don't give up. There's another half to play.' "

"You know what that's like, huh?" a student quips.

There he goes again, I think, cutting down the nets in practice. He really believes that his team can beat anybody, and now his team is playing for some real stakes.

"Hey, Coach," another student says, "you could be spending the rest of your life on a golf course."

Dick laughs (a little ruefully I think). "No, I'm going back in the cities for the kids I left behind."

A brief update: Dillon James Moyer was born on July 18, 1991, and is the apple of his grandparents' eyes. Dick's father died just before Thanksgiving. He never really recovered from his operation the winter before and his health deteriorated. He died at home, just one hour after Karen, Jamie, and Dillon arrived at their house for Thanksgiving: he died with his granddaughter and great-grandson praying at his side.

LaPhonso Ellis dropped his accounting major and has been eligible all year. The Notre Dame football team played in the Sugar Bowl against Florida—Notre Dame came out in green uniforms, Florida wears orange, no one said anything about Ireland.

I love living in London and Dick and I have been able to spend time together, the most ever in one period in our lives, touring the city, visiting the incredible cathedrals in Winchester and Canterbury, going to plays and art museums. Dick follows Notre Dame basketball closely, genuinely happy when they win. The only time he was upset this year was when a South Bend reporter wrote that the program had been left in disarray and the present players had no talent, or very little. A few big wins after some unexpected early losses stilled that kind of talk and Dick is hoping Notre Dame receives a tournament bid. He is also hoping that LaPhonso will be, if not an accountant, a first-round draft pick.

I ignore basketball altogether. I don't miss not being recognized anymore and only the occasional American recognizes Dick. I'm finding that I like administrative work and I'm particularly pleased to be able to work with a small group of students rather than the hundreds at the South Bend campus. Karen and Dillon have been to visit and we took Dillon to Buckingham Palace to see the queen. He slept through it and she was not at home. The trip was, nonetheless, a success. Rick and Jenny, Mary and Fred Ferlic with their children, Chris Nee, Mary Ann and Jim Roemer, and many other friends are coming to visit so I have little time to brood. When I do think about basketball at all, I think that we will years hence look back on college sports of the nineties much as we look back on the Wall Street of the eighties. How had we so lost our values? What forces blinded us to our excesses and our greed?

The past never completely disappears though. Maureen and Vince Kempton unexpectedly appeared in my office one day. They stopped off in London on their way home from visiting Tim in Italy where he plays basketball. They had heard I was directing the law school and looked me up. And in late January Dick and I traveled to Belgium for the weekend. We were having tea in the lobby of a large hotel in Antwerp when Dick spotted a familiar face. "Varner!" he yelled in his best practice voice. Billy Varner, who played for Dick in the early eighties and now plays in Belgium, jumped, wondering what he had done wrong. He turned around, spotted us, and greeted us as long-lost parents. "I thought I was dreaming when I hear that voice yell 'Varner!' " he said later. "No, not exactly dreaming, more like having a nightmare. I'd blown a move again and Coach was about to get on me." Billy brought his wife and little girl to the hotel to meet us and showed up at the airport on Sunday laden with gifts to see us off to London. His nostalgia for the past and his open affection for us go a long way in healing the wounds of the final year.

Last year seems very far away; the pettiness of campus and athletic politics seems trivial and unimportant. Sometimes I feel a little anxious about the uncertainty of our future. Our lives were so fixed, so regulated for so long. It is like all the seasons ending at once. We are gypsies and must adjust to what looks like a vagabond life once more. We're working out how to live in the same city or at least the same country for a while. At those times I ponder the unfinished quilt of my life and see only the frayed ends on the underside. Most times, though, I know we are just works-in-progress, and we may never understand how the pattern is supposed to turn out. Perhaps it's the very age of things over here, the ongoing sense, as at Stonehenge, that lives and centuries have passed and we are but a small part of a very long story.

One basketball memory lingers. We were with the basketball team in Yugoslavia, on a tour that the NCAA permits college teams to go on every four years. Our last trip to Italy and Spain in 1975 had been filled with misadventures and culminated in our abandonment in Madrid, with fifteen disgruntled players and nowhere to go.

We had traveled in 1979 to Yugoslavia, not knowing what to expect. A week later we were in love with the country, with its people, with everything about it. Although the accommodations were frequently not pristine according to American standards, the charm and friendliness of the people won us over forever. Much of Yugoslavia seemed untouched by the twentieth century and that, of course, is a mixed blessing. One night, playing in a small town somewhere south of Belgrade, Orlando Woolridge shattered the glass backboard during the pregame warm-ups. The sudden explosion of glass caught the glow from the overhead arena lights and showered down on the amazed players, like a fireworks display in slow motion. Miraculously, no one was hurt. Two maintenance men, with ancient brooms and pails, slowly began to sweep the glass away. After about an hour of ineffectual cleanup and attempts to replace the backboard, we adjourned to an outside playground, which had a few stands and some lights, to play the game. In this country of few victories, success on the basketball court had marshaled national pride. No matter what, the basketball game must go on. As I sat in the shaky stands, under a few feeble lights, two children shyly approached me with a huge bouquet of flowers, a gift from the town, to honor the wife of the coach from the United States. For that moment, and so many others like it, I loved being a coach's wife.